LOSS CONTROL FOR THE SMALL TO MEDIUM SIZE BUSINESS

Reducing Workers' Compensation Costs

ROBERT E. BRISBIN

VNR VAN NOSTRAND REINHOLD
New York

Copyright © 1990 by Van Nostrand Reinhold

Library of Congress Catalog Card Number 89-16478
ISBN 0-442-23945-9

Printed in the United States of America

HD
7103.65
U6
B75
1990

Van Nostrand Reinhold
115 Fifth Avenue
New York, New York 10003

Van Nostrand Reinhold International Company Limited
11 New Fetter Lane
London EC4P 4EE, England

Van Nostrand Reinhold
480 La Trobe Street
Melbourne, Victoria 3000, Australia

Nelson Canada
1120 Birchmount Road
Scarborough, Ontario M1K 5G4, Canada

16 15 14 13 12 11 10 9 8 7 6 5 4 3 2 1

Library of Congress Cataloging-in-Publication Data

Brisbin, Robert E., 1946-
    Loss control for the small to medium size business: reducing
workers' compensation costs/Robert E. Brisbin.
        p. cm.
    Bibliography: p.
    Includes index.
    ISBN 0-442-23945-9
    1. Workers' compensation--United States--Cost control.
    2. Industrial safety--United States.   I. Title.
    HD7103.65.U6B75   1990
    658.15′53--dc20   89-16478
                                                                              CIP

TO: ELMO JOSEPH
KEN TAYLOR
SALLY BRISBIN
CHARLES AND MONICA HULL

CONTENTS

PREFACE

This book is designed to provide a guide to establishing an effective loss control program for the small and medium size business. The purpose of the book is to help employers reduce their workers' compensation insurance costs.

All the material in this book is based on successful methods that have been proved under actual working conditions. The information is specific and can be put into practice to reach the individual employer's desired goals. The emphasis is on identifying the critical point of control, presenting the principles and procedures necessary to effect the control, and providing practical solutions to common loss control problems.

If loss control is to be efficient and effective, all procedures and principles of the program must be smoothly integrated. Experience has shown that success can best be achieved when specific requirements are met and a successful sequence of steps followed. In general, the order of the material in this book illustrates a successful sequence.

In addition, the text contains specific topics for safety meetings that should help readers to think of other topics more relevant to their individual operations.

A Resource section on sources of information and additional loss control material includes names, addresses and telephone numbers to contact for answers to many loss control and safety questions. A chapter on miscellaneous loss control ideas is designed to stimulate thought about areas that are often overlooked. Here the reader will also find a list of questions commonly asked by insurance underwriters, with an explanation of what specific information is sought and why it is applicable to the decision being made to accept or deny the employer's application for workers' compensation insurance coverage.

An insurance crisis exists in this country. The costs of purchasing insurance and resolving claims continue to escalate at an alarming rate. Nowhere are these costs felt more directly than in the purchase of workers' compensation insurance by an employer. Unlike other forms of insurance, workers' compensation, by law, must be purchased by every employer in the United States. In some states, employers have the option of purchasing workers' compensation insurance from private carriers or from state-funded insurance programs. In other states, the only option is a state-funded program. Regardless of the type of insurance available to any given employer, the guidelines presented in this book will provide the employer with a method of controlling and reducing that portion of workers' compensation costs which may be addressed by direct management involvement.

INTRODUCTION

Loss control may be defined as policies and procedures undertaken by an employer to reduce and/or eliminate the factors that cause worker injuries or raise workers' compensation insurance costs. The employer who succeeds in establishing an effective loss control program gains the additional benefits of improved efficiency, increased profits, and the development of a strong bond between employer and employees.

Workers' compensation insurance costs have a significant effect on the profitability of any business. This effect is both direct and indirect: The direct costs include premiums paid for workers' compensation insurance, costs incurred by the employer as the result of medical treatment and rehabilitation, and the increased costs of hiring replacement personnel during the recovery period of an injured employee. As significant as these costs are, the indirect costs are even more expensive, though hidden. They include reduced efficiency of production due to lowered morale following a serious accident, and increased training costs associated with the training of new personnel hired to replace injured workers. Hidden costs represent from four to five times the cost of direct expenses resulting from worker injuries.

Employers have a tendency to measure workers' compensation costs strictly as a factor of premiums paid less dividends received from insurance carriers where participating plans are in effect. But an emphasis on dividend receipts can be extremely misleading in regard to actual net costs.

All states use a rating system for determining workers' compensation insurance premiums based on job classifications with rates per $100 of payroll per job class. The job classification reflects the relative hazard associated with the work performed. For example, the rate for a carpenter may be $30 per $100 of payroll, while the rate for a retail store clerk may be only $1.50 per $100 of payroll.

These rates (also known as the *manual premium*) are then modified by the actual injury or loss experience of each employer. This modification of rates per $100 of payroll is known as an *experience modifier*. The experience modifier modifies the established manual premium rates upward or downward, depending upon the loss record of the individual employer.

Loss statistics are collected by the state regulatory department charged with establishing workers' compensation insurance experience modifiers. These statistics are derived from the loss report databases of all insurance carriers operating within the state for each individual employer. In the following example, payrolls and job classifications are assumed to be about equal.

- If a payroll develops a manual premium of $17,250 with a 1.38 experience modifier, the total annual premium will be $23,805. With a dividend of $10,005, the net cost is $13,800.
- If a payroll develops a manual premium of $17,250 with a 1.02 experience modifier, the total annual premium will be $17,595. With a dividend of $4,526 the net cost is $13,069.
- If a payroll develops a manual premium of $17,250 with a 0.75 experience modifier, the total annual premium will be $12,938. With a dividend of $2,616, the net cost is $10,322.

As these examples show, the amount of dividend received is not the critical factor in determining the net cost of workers' compensation insurance. The net costs are directly related to the experience modifier used to establish annual premiums. And the experience modifier is directly related to the effectiveness of the employer's loss control program.

Furthermore, remember that dividends are not paid until at least 12 months after the close of the policy year in which they have accrued. The employer in the first example has put out substantially more capital for workers' compensation insurance premiums than the employer in the third example. This increased payment of premium dollars means higher negative cash flows including, in some instances, interest payments if the premium money is borrowed. At the very least, less capital is available for reinvestment in the business.

The following chapters will take you step by step through the process of developing an effective loss control program. The effectiveness of your particular program depends on the results as a whole, like a puzzle which is complete only when all the pieces are in their proper place. The complete picture has greater impact than any one piece alone.

Employers often make the mistake of implementing only a portion of the needed loss control procedures, those they consider most important. Unfortunately, the resulting net costs, when compared to those of employers who have developed the entire program, show the error of shortsighted thinking.

1

THE WRITTEN FRAMEWORK

The first step in establishing a formal loss control program is to develop a written framework within which to conduct loss control activities. A written framework focuses the attention of all employees on the importance of a safety-conscious attitude and a safe work enviroment. A written framework also serves as proof of management's desire to provide a safe working enviroment for all employees. While labor law varies considerably from state to state, all states require an employer to establish an effective safety program and to supervise employees to ensure that safe operating practices are followed.

Documentation of the safety program may or may not be required by law. However, should the company find itself in a position of needing to prove in a court of law that it does have a safe operating practices policy in place, it will be hard pressed to prove that such a policy is in effect without solid documentation.

The basic written framework should consist of the following items:

- A written statement of safety policy (Exhibit 1-1).
- Written rules and regulations for employees to follow (Exhibit 1-2).

- A statement of compliance signed by all employees indicating their willingness to comply with company safety efforts (Exhibit 1-3).

Loss control efforts are only as effective as top management's willingness to communicate the necessity for a zero loss enviroment. Middle managers and employees will perform their duties in accordance with the signals sent by top management because they know that their advancement within the company, and indeed the security of their jobs, is dependent on their performing to the standards set by top management.

Promulgating a policy only to negate it through management actions that signal to employees that loss control is not a priority is a complete waste of time and money. Policy enforcement is essential for the success of the policy. Employees must always know the boundaries within which they are to operate. For this reason, written rules and regulations are necessary. It is a good idea to limit rules and regulations for policy puposes to general safety areas. This will leave enough flexibility to allow individual supervisors to conduct their operations in the safest and most efficient manner. Specific operational rules should be reserved for training manuals and checklists.

One of the pitfalls of documentation is that it can be used as a double-edged sword by attorneys attacking the employer. When written rules for general safety policy purposes are too specific—addressing particular machine operations, for example—they create a degree of authority above and beyond that which should be provided by the general policy statement. If a particular operation, machine, or procedure is changed or added, the entire policy must be revised to include the new criteria. If it is not revised, an attorney may then point out that the policy is severely deficient, thus negating the defense value of documentation.

Specific procedures and operations should be covered in training documents such as checklists, manuals, safety meetings, and individual consultations. Training criteria are discussed in Chapter 7.

COMPANY SAFETY POLICY

(On Company Letterhead)

(*Name of Company*) considers the prevention of accidents an important part of its operation. We are vitally concerned with the human suffering and considerable financial loss resulting from accidents on the job. The prevention of accidents is therefore of major importance to the company, and the active, full cooperation of all employees is required.

You are expected to play a definite part in our safety program; it will not succeed without your cooperation. This will include attending job safety meetings and adhering strictly to all written and commonsense rules and regulations governing safe operations. It is part of the company safety policy that no job being performed is so important that there is not enough time to do the work the right way—the safe way.

Safety rules are attached and are to be complied with. We welcome suggestions to help improve our safety standards.

Signature ——————————— Date ————————

Exhibit 1-1

GENERAL SAFETY RULES

(Customize and Place on
Company Letterhead)

You are working for an organization that is sincere in its desire to conduct all its operations in the safest manner possible. Compliance with the General Safety Rules listed below will assist us in achieving this objective. These rules are minimum guides for working safely. Your awareness and cooperation in loss control is a vital part of your job. It is your duty to follow all accepted standards of loss control.

1. Whenever you are involved in any accident that results in personal injury or damage to property, no matter how small, the accident must be reported. Get first aid promptly.

2. Report immediately any condition or practice you think might cause injury or damage to equipment.

3. Do not operate any equipment which, in your opinion, is not in a safe condition.

4. All prescribed safety and personal protective equipment should be used when required and maintained in a safe working condition.

5. Obey all company rules, governmental regulations, signs, markings, and instructions. Be familiar with those that apply directly to you. If you don't know why—ask!

6. When lifting, use the approved lifting technique—i.e., bend your knees, grasp the load firmly, lift with your legs.

7. Don't engage in horseplay; avoid distracting others; be courteous.

8. Always use the right tools and equipment for the job. Use them safely and only when authorized.

Exhibit 1-2

9. Good housekeeping should always be practiced. Return all tools, equipment, materials, etc., to their proper places. Disorder wastes time, energy, and material, and will often result in injury.
10. The use of drugs and/or intoxicating beverages is prohibited.
11. All employees will follow instructions and safe operating procedures as directed by their supervisors. Failure to comply with a supervisor's instruction may be cause for immediate termination.

Signature _____ Date _____

Exhibit 1-2 (*cont.*)

STATEMENT OF COMPLIANCE WITHOUT INCENTIVE PROGRAM

(Place on Company Letterhead)

THIS IS TO CERTIFY that I have received and read the company's safety policy.

I understand it is one of the requirements of my employment that in the event I am injured while in the course of my work, I will report immediately to my supervisor and obtain any first aid or medical treatment necessary. I understand that all accidents, regardless of their severity, will be investigated.

Signature ———————————— Date ————————

Exhibit 1-3(a)

STATEMENT OF COMPLIANCE WITH SAFETY INCENTIVE PROGRAM

(Place on Company Letterhead)

THIS IS TO CERTIFY that I have received and read the company's safety policy.

I understand that it is one of the requirements of my employment that in the event I am injured while in the course of my work, I will report immediately to my supervisor and obtain any first aid or medical treatment necessary. I further understand that all accidents, regardless of how minor, must be reported immediately to my supervisor, even if reporting such an accident would disqualify me from receiving a safety incentive bonus during the month in which the accident occurs. I understand that all accidents, regardless of severity, will be investigated.

Signature _____ Date _____

Exhibit 1-3(b)

Once top management has established the safety policy and the basic operating rules, it is necessary to obtain a statement of compliance from employees. Such a statement serves two purposes:

- It creates a mutually beneficial contract between the employee and the company. Everyone tends to take more seriously a contract that is written and that applies to safety and the employee as well. It further reinforces in the mind of the employee that top management considers safe operations and zero accidents very important.
- It provides documentation that the employee has been informed of company loss control procedures and has agreed to comply with these procedures. This documentation will be critical to the chain of evidence necessary to defend against discriminatory practices lawsuits should it become necessary to discipline an employee for noncompliance with loss control procedures.

2

CHOOSING A SAFETY DIRECTOR

THE SAFETY DIRECTOR

Choosing the company safety director is a critical aspect of developing an effective loss control program. The safety director will motivate all your employees to become safety-conscious, and a safety-conscious attitude is the single most important factor in reducing and avoiding work-related injuries.

By regulation every company, regardless of size, must have a person responsible for employee safety. In small firms, this person is generally the production manager or the owner. However, it should not be assumed that because an individual performs well in meeting production goals that he or she will also be an ideal candidate for safety director.

The safety director is the channel through which policy and corrective action flows from the top down and suggestions for improvement flow from line employees up to management. The safety director is responsible for investigating all accidents and determining the company's position on the validity of each claim so that appropriate steps may be taken by the insurance carrier to protect company interests. More dollars are spent in resolving litigated workers' compensation claims than in benefits provided to injured workers. In 80 percent of the questionable claims cases, litigation would not have been successful if the company had provided its insurance carrier with timely, accurate information.

Important Traits

There are specific traits which make a safety director effective or ineffective:

- The safety director cannot be someone whose attitude is that accidents are caused by stupidity, or that a zero accident rate cannot be reached because accidents "just happen" from time to time.
- The safety director must have an open mind, be concerned about the welfare of other employees, and have a strong desire to reach the goal of zero accidents.
- The ideal person must be well organized. Choosing someone whose work station consistently looks like a disaster area will result in failure. Organization and the ability to cope with changing situations are essential to success.
- The safety director should command the respect of other workers and subordinates. This natural leadership ability must be augmented by the wholehearted support of executive management.
- The safety director needs to have the authority to enforce safe operating procedures and implement reasonable operating changes where appropriate.
- The safety director must be capable of conducting safety meetings. Choosing someone who is unable to speak to a group will only lead to procrastination and ineffectiveness.
- The safety director needs to have good verbal and written communication skills.
- The safety director must be capable of conducting an accident investigation, interviewing witnesses, recommending corrective action, and putting all the above into coherent written form for future reference. Obviously the safety director cannot be someone who hates paperwork.
- The safety director must be capable of looking ahead, and of making every effort to foresee hazards inherent in a new

operation. He or she must be able to supervise the development and implementation of appropriate new procedures.

An employer will often fail to identify an employee with the requisite talent for being a safety director. The tendency is simply to heap further responsibility on the most available generalist manager. While it is true that whoever is chosen should be familiar with all phases of the operation and communicate regularly with all departments, it is pointless to give more responsibility to an already overworked employee.

Duties of the Safety Director

Here are the usual duties a safety director performs:

- Conducts safety inspections, including counseling employees, directing supervisors to train employees in specific tasks, identifying the need for safety-related equipment and receiving authorization for procurement, channeling safety suggestions from line employees and supervisors to management for authorization to implement, keeping records of safety inspections and completion dates of corrective actions.
- Ensures that safety meetings are held by conducting the meetings and/or assigning topics/dates to supervisors; maintains records of safety meetings.
- Ensures that training is conducted and documented.
- Conducts accident investigations, takes witness and claimant statements, assures corrective action is taken, forwards all documentation for filing with the insurance carrier.
- Develops safety incentive programs, keeps abreast of changes in safety regulations that could have an effect on company operations, keeps informed of safety advances, improvements, and procedures.

3

DEVELOPING A SAFETY INSPECTION PROGRAM

Regular safety inspections are required by OSHA (Occupational Safety and Health Administration) regulations. Safety inspections are an excellent management tool for determining where to concentrate safety efforts, and for identifying potential accident causes before they result in injury to a worker. Corrective action taken prior to an injury is the most cost-effective way to apply lessons normally learned only after an injury occurs.

Regardless of how much time and effort is put into safety training, employees will need to be reminded, and in some cases repeatedly trained, to ensure that safe operating procedures are routinely followed. Lapses of concentration, production deadlines, and old habits conspire to erode the effectiveness of safety training and safe operating practices. A documented safety inspection program provides an opportunity to review a series of past safety inspections to determine those areas and/or employees in need of safety training and counseling. No other tool is as effective.

The safety inspection program begins with a walk around the premises by the safety director to identify potential injury areas and operations. Each area or operation with such potential is an ideal inspection checkpoint. Fixed safety areas such as fire extinguishers, fire doors, firefighting equipment, first aid equipment, and machine guards are also excellent inspection checkpoints. Reviewing past injury reports and corrective action will reveal additional checkpoints. Once areas of concern are identified, a safety inspection checklist can be designed.

Safety inspections should be conducted weekly, with the day of the week and the hour of the day the inspection is conducted rotated. The routine questions on the checklist are only a portion of the inspection process. The inspectors must use their own initiative to look for other hazards that may cause injury and can be corrected.

The checklist should be not more than two pages long. Obviously some operations may require a more extensive list, but the shorter the checklist, the more effective the inspection (Exhibits 3-1 to 3-6). This is because a longer list will cause the inspector to rely on checkpoints alone instead of observation. Hazards in operating areas ebb and flow depending on worker concentration and fatigue levels. Normally benign areas can be points of major concern under the right circumstances, so observation is important.

Additional comments should be routine on the completed inspection form. Inspections without any comments are highly unusual and generally indicate that the inspection was not thorough. If an employee is observed following improper procedures, a counseling talk should be held immediately to correct the problem. This discussion should be documented in the additional comments section, and the signature of the employee obtained to indicate that the counseling session took place. If corrective action requires physical changes, always note on the inspection form an estimated date for completion, and on a future inspection, the date of actual completion.

Completed safety inspections should be filed and reviewed every six weeks to see if patterns of problems or repeated procedural errors are being noted. Problems found during safety inspections make excellent topics for weekly safety meetings.

WEEKLY SAFETY INSPECTION:
CONSTRUCTION JOBSITES DATE

Date   OK   Correct

1. All personnel wearing   _____   _____
   appropriate personal protection
   (Goggles, hard hats, gloves,
   etc.)?
2. All tools being properly used?   _____   _____
3. Right tools for job being   _____   _____
   performed?
4. Appropriate procedures being   _____   _____
   followed?
5. All holes on job site covered?   _____   _____
6. All trenches properly shored?   _____   _____
7. All tools properly guarded?   _____   _____
8. All personal working above   _____   _____
   ground level followng proper
   safety procedures?
9. Is job site housekeeping   _____   _____
   satisfactory?
10. First aid kit fully stocked?   _____   _____
    Emergency medical aid available
    and method of calling known to
    all?

Additional observations and corrective action taken:

REMIND YOUR PEOPLE TO THINK ABOUT SAFE
PROCEDURES BEFORE AND DURING THE
PERFORMANCE OF ANY OPERATION.

Exhibit 3-1

WEEKLY SAFETY INSPECTION: EXCAVATION SITES

Date   YES   NO

1. All personnel wearing proper protective equipment? (gloves, goggles, etc.)   _____   _____
2. Air brake pressures checked?   _____   _____
3. Backup alarms working?   _____   _____
4. Proper procedures followed?   _____   _____
5. Holes on job site covered?   _____   _____
6. Trenches properly shored?   _____   _____
7. Have cranes been inspected and certified?   _____   _____
8. Personnel following safety procedures?   _____   _____
9. Housekeeping at site good?   _____   _____
10. First aid kit stocked?   _____   _____
11. Method of calling emergency medical aid known?   _____   _____

Additional observations:

Corrective action taken:

Signature _____ Date _____

REMIND YOUR PEOPLE TO THINK ABOUT SAFETY PROCEDURES BEFORE AND DURING THE PERFORMANCE OF ANY OPERATION.

Exhibit 3-2

MANUFACTURER'S WEEKLY SAFETY INSPECTION CHECKLIST

Date		YES	NO
1.	Are all employees following proper procedures?	_____	_____
2.	Are all employees wearing appropriate protective equipment?	_____	_____
3.	Housekeeping satisfactory?	_____	_____
4.	Housekeeping in storage areas satisfactory?	_____	_____
5.	Obsolete parts and scrap removed daily?	_____	_____
6.	Are fire extinguishers marked and accessible?	_____	_____
7.	Are circuit breakers accessible?	_____	_____
8.	Do grinders have eye protection and warning signs adjacent to their location?	_____	_____
9.	Are acetylene regulators and hoses off the ground?	_____	_____
10.	Are all employees working at jobs they have been checked out on?	_____	_____
11.	First aid kits stocked and available?	_____	_____
12.	Supervisory personnel know how to call emergency medical aid?	_____	_____

Additional comments:

Corrective action taken:

Signature _____ Date _____

Exhibit 3-3

RESTAURANT WEEKLY SAFETY
INSPECTION CHECKLIST

Date   YES   NO

1. Are all employees following
   proper procedures?   _____   _____
2. Are all employees wearing
   appropriate clothing?   _____   _____
3. Housekeeping satisfactory?   _____   _____
4. Housekeeping in storage areas
   satisfactory?   _____   _____
5. Spills, other slip hazards
   cleaned up?   _____   _____
6. Are knives properly stored?   _____   _____
7. Are slicer guards in place? At
   zero?   _____   _____
8. Are employees trying to work
   too fast?   _____   _____
9. Are all nonslip mats in place?   _____   _____
10. Are all employees working at
    jobs they have been checked
    out on?   _____   _____
11. First aid kits stocked and
    available?   _____   _____
12. Supervisory personnel know how
    to call emergency
    medical aid?   _____   _____

Additional comments:

Corrective action taken:

Signature _____ Date _____

Exhibit 3-4

SCAFFOLD SAFETY CHECKLIST

Date   YES   NO

1. Are footings stable, soundly set?   _____   _____
2. Are guardrails installed on all
    open sides?   _____   _____
3. Are guardrails installed on all
    open ends?   _____   _____
4. Any damaged or obviously
    weakened members?   _____   _____
5. All planking overlapped at least
    12 inches?   _____   _____
6. Does planking fill entire space
    between wall and guardrails?   _____   _____
7. Are access ladders provided?   _____   _____
8. Any single boards used for
    access?   _____   _____
9. Are workers wearing hard hats
    where needed?   _____   _____
10. Are scaffolds secured to wall at
    least every 25 feet?   _____   _____

Additional comments:

Inspected by: _____

Discussed with: _____

NOTE TO SUPERVISOR

It must not be assumed that every unsafe condition or procedure has been covered in this or any prior inspection, Further, we make no representation nor assume any responsibility that locations, workplaces, operations, machinery, and equipment are safe, or healthful, or in compliance with any law, rule, or regulation.

Exhibit 3-5

AUTO REPAIR FACILITY: WEEKLY SAFETY INSPECTION CHECKLIST

Date   YES   NO

1. Are all employees following
    proper procedures?   _____   _____
2. Are all employees wearing
    appropriate protective
    equipment?   _____   _____
3. Housekeeping satisfactory?   _____   _____
4. Any spills or trip and fall
    hazards?   _____   _____
5. Obsolete parts and scrap
    removed daily?   _____   _____
6. Are fire extinguishers marked
    and accesible?   _____   _____
7. Are circuit breakers accessible?   _____   _____
8. Do grinders have eye protection
    and warning signs adjacent to
    their location?   _____   _____
9. Are air hoses off the ground
    when not in use?   _____   _____
10. Are all employees working at
    jobs they have been checked
    out on?   _____   _____
11. First aid kits stocked and
    available?   _____   _____
12. Are safety glasses being worn
    where needed?   _____   _____

Additional comments:

Corrective action taken:

Signature _____ Date _____

Exhibit 3-6

VEHICLE CHECKLIST

Date	OK	NEEDS ATTENTION
Battery	____	_____
Brakes	____	_____
Brake lights & turn signals	____	_____
Hand brake	____	_____
Hoses, belts, connections	____	_____
Body & glass (check for damage)	____	_____
Trailer hitch	____	_____
Emergency equipment	____	_____
Cab housekeeping	____	_____
Mirrors	____	_____
Instruments and gauges	____	_____
Steering	____	_____
Tie downs	____	_____
Tires (air pressure, tread, damage)	____	_____
Oil	____	_____

Comments:

Signature _____   Date _____

Exhibit 3-7

GENERAL SAFETY INSPECTION

Date   YES   NO

1. OSHA Form 200 up to date?   _____   _____
2. Loss control documentation
    current?   _____   _____
3. Emergency plans current?   _____   _____
4. Hazcom training & binder
    current?   _____   _____
5. Any trip and fall hazards?   _____   _____
6. Gas cylinders secured?   _____   _____
7. Flammables stored properly?   _____   _____
8. Protective equipment inventory
    current?   _____   _____
9. Lockout tags used? Inventory?   _____   _____
10. Eyewash station filled & current? _____   _____
11. Fire extinguishers mounted,
    signed, current?   _____   _____
12. Machine guards in place?   _____   _____
13. Electrical wiring adequate?   _____   _____
14. Extension cords used properly?   _____   _____
15. All circuit breakers labeled?   _____   _____
16. All hazardous materials labeled? _____   _____

Additional comments:

Signature _____ Date _____

Exhibit 3-8

FLEET VEHICLE INSPECTIONS

Where company vehicles are driven by employees either on or off site, regular documented safety inspections should be performed by the assigned driver. These inspections should be performed daily, but documented by the driver at least weekly and the documents turned into the safety director.

The documented vehicle safety inspection should be reviewed by the safety director each week and any mechanical problems corrected as soon as possible. To assure accuracy, the safety director should conduct a vehicle inspection at random on a rotating basis, making certain that all vehicles are inspected by the safety director at least every 6 months (Exhibits 3-7 and 3-8).

Each driver should have his or her driver's license record reviewed on an annual basis, as well as before hiring, to ensure that drivers meet and continue to meet company safe driving standards.

Where vehicle allowances are provided to employees or actual fleets are maintained, it is essential that the company develop a well-defined, documented vehicle and driver policy with statements of willingness to comply signed by all drivers prior to vehicle assignment. It is beyond the scope of this book to provide an example of a company vehicle policy. However, assistance can be obtained from the traffic safety departments of most local law enforcement agencies, state highway patrol agencies, or the loss control department of the company insurance carrier.

4

CONDUCTING SAFETY MEETINGS

The single most important factor in avoiding work-related injuries is instilling a safety-conscious attitude in the minds of your employees. Following safe operating procedures is an approach that prevents a worker from being injured at any time, on or off the job. With very few exceptions, injuries have been contributed to by the injured party, because of unsafe operating procedures or poor planning. The safety meeting is an appropriate tool for helping to instill a safety-conscious attitude. Safety meetings should last no longer than 15 minutes. Personal presentations by the employees themselves and by supervisors are more effective. Showing films or slides is least effective. Topics for discussion may be derived from a variety of sources, including prior safety inspections.

Involvement of line employees in the safety meeting is very effective. Assigning a topic to an employee and having the employee present the topic to co-workers provides positive recognition to the chosen employee, fixes the topic in the mind of the employee, and is a most effective way to gain the attention of other employees at the meeting because the speaker is a peer.

Small, frequent safety meetings are much more effective then large or infrequent meetings. The least effective safety meeting is large, infrequent, and involves using a film, or slides. Meetings should be held at least once a month. They are required in the construction industry at the job site at least every 10 days. Ideally, safety meetings should be held once a week.

Safety meetings should always be documented with the date of the meeting, the topic of discussion, and the signatures of employees in attendance. Writing down an employee's name does not prove that the employee attended the meeting. There have been successful lawsuits by employees seeking additional benefits because the employer did not train or warn an employee of a hazard on the job. A signed report of a safety meeting at which the hazard which led to an injury was discussed would be very helpful in the employer's defense.

TOPIC SOURCES

Local Safety Councils will often have available a list of safety topics, and/or sources of topics. Here are some sources:

- The National Safety Council
- State Occupational Safety and Health administrations
- Federal Occupational Safety and Health Administration
- American Society of Safety Engineers
- Safety Meeting Outlines, Inc. (see Sources section)
- Manufacturers of equipment used in your operation
- Safety inspections you have conducted
- Past injury reports from your own files

Exhibits 4-1 through 4-28 present samples of good safety meeting reports on a variety of topics.

SAFETY MEETING REPORT

Date:

Conducted by:

Make certain all systems are working properly on vehicles. Set parking brake when parked even for short periods.

"Welders" make certain fittings on equipment are tight. Combustible material must be cleared from area before using cutting torch or welding apparatus.

Gasoline should never be used for cleaning.

Extension cords can create a trip and fall hazard. Cords should be returned to the shop when work is finished.

Stack materials safely. An accident caused by negligence can lead to civil or criminal penalties for the guilty party.

Use respiratory protective equipment whenever there is respiratory exposure.

Anyone injured on the job and requiring medical attention must be accompanied to the doctor. No injured employee should be allowed to drive himself or herself to a medical facility.

Additional comments:

Attended by:

Exhibit 4-1

SAFETY MEETING REPORT

Date:

Conducted by:

Everyone has times when they feel the pressure of tight scheduling. During those times, it may seem as though a shortcut is worth taking. However, a shortcut may jeopardize the safety of a worker. An injured worker will put you much further behind schedule. An accident is never worth risking.

Horseplay is an unsafe act which will have an adverse influence on safety and is prohibited.

Additional comments:

Attended by:

Exhibit 4-2

SAFETY MEETING REPORT

Date:

Conducted by:

Topic: Eye and face protection

Any worker who is grinding, drilling, chipping, burning, or who may be in an area that has a heavy concentration of dust must wear safety glasses, goggles, or a face shield.

There is a reason for eye protection. Once your eyes are damaged, there is no replacing them.

Never throw objects from heights without seeing that proper steps have been taken to protect others from the falling hazard.

Wear sturdy work shoes; sneakers, running shoes, etc. will not be allowed.

Plan ahead. Know exactly what you are going to do before starting to perform your job safely.

Additional comments:

Attended by:

Exhibit 4-3

SAFETY MEETING REPORT

Date:
Conducted by:
Topic: The key to safety

Supervisors must set a good example and show safe operating procedures. When safety is ignored, injuries occur. The employee depends upon supervision for good leadership and safety.

Always return tools and equipment to their proper place when you are through using them. Tools lying around create a safety hazard.

Lock out the power source before performing maintenance.

Do not use stepladders with loose steps and broken side rails. If one is found, turn it in for replacement or repair.

Additional comments:

Attended by:

Exhibit 4-4

SAFETY MEETING REPORT

Date:

Conducted by:

Topic: Extension ladders

When setting up extension ladders, check the condition of the ladder to make sure that rungs, side rails, and feet are in good condition.

When setting up the ladder, the base should be one-fourth the length from the vertical plane of the top support and 36 inches above the top support to the end of the ladder.

Tie the ladder off so it is secure.

Additional comments:

Attended by:

Exhibit 4-5

SAFETY MEETING REPORT

Date:
Conducted by:
Topic: Scaffolding

When constructing a scaffold, make sure all braces, toe-boards, handrails, and midrails are in place.

Use 2″ × 10″ planks laid close together. The length should overlap the ledgers at each end by at least 6 inches. Nailing cleats of 1 inch wood on the underside of each projecting end inside the ledgers will keep the planks from sliding off.

Always tie scaffolding off to the structural steel to prevent it from swaying or collapsing.

Do not work from unapproved scaffolds.

Keep scaffolds clear of miscellaneous debris. Items not properly stored or tied down can be knocked off, or cause a slip and fall accident.

Proper access to and from the scaffold must be provided.

Rope off the area below overhead work and keep everyone out.

Tie off power tools when working overhead.

Additional comments:

Attended by:

Exhibit 4-6

SAFETY MEETING REPORT

Date:
Conducted by:
Topic: Lift with your legs

Your back muscles were not made for lifting. Your legs have the strongest muscles in your body. Stand close to the load, feet apart; squat down and lift slowly. Keep your back as straight as possible. Stand up with the load, using your legs. This will place as little strain as possible on the back. If your assignment requires turning in the direction you wish to go, do not twist the upper body while holding the load.

Both hands should securely hold the load before you start to lift. If it is a box that you are lifting, grip the corners diagonally for better balance.

Keep all areas clear of debris to avoid tripping with the load.

Additional comments:

Attended by:

Exhibit 4-7

SAFETY MEETING REPORT

Date:
Conducted by:
Topic: Safety is good business

Each employee must take it upon himself or herself to look for unsafe conditions and correct them.

Accidents can result in lost time from work, lead to other health problems, and cause permanent disability. Remember equipment can be repaired, but a person may not always recover completely.

Housekeeping is a continuous job. It requires a constant effort, on a daily basis. Keep all areas clean and free of debris. Ignoring trash leads to ignoring safe operating procedures and that will lead to an accident.

When working in reduced light conditions, get proper lighting.

Additional comments:

Attended by:

Exhibit 4-8

SAFETY MEETING REPORT

Date:
Conducted by:
Topic: A safety-conscious attitude

The need to develop a safety-conscious attitude cannot be overemphasized because a safety-conscious attitude is the only sure way to prevent injuries and accidents.

Having a safety-conscious attitude is more than just showing up at work and putting on protective equipment, or making sure your machine guards are in place.

Having a safety-conscious attitude is thinking about the job you will be doing and the hazards that are associated with that job before you start working.

Having a safety-conscious attitude is making a firm decision that you will always operate in a safe manner and that you will concentrate on the job at hand. You will make certain that every procedure required is performed in a safe manner.

Having a safety-conscious attitude is taking the time to get the proper personal protective equipment and to put it on, even if it takes longer to find than it will take to complete the job. The worker who is too lazy to find a pair of safety glasses before using the grinder does not have a safety-conscious attitude. The time it takes to loose your eyesight cannot be measured in seconds, but the time it takes to remember how foolish you were not to have put on those glasses is a lifetime.

Having a safety-conscious attitude is not just a matter of not wanting to get hurt, but a matter of having the pride and self-respect to do the job the way it is supposed to be done. That is, the safe way.

I would like to open this meeting for a discussion. Specifically, I would like each of you to tell me what you have done today, or what you will do today to ensure that you have a safety-conscious attitude.

Attended by:

Exhibit 4-9

SAFETY MEETING REPORT

Date:

Conducted by:

Topic: Back injuries

There are basically two types of back injuries:

1. Those that occur to the spinal column
2. Those that occur to the back muscles

The spinal column consists of vertebrae which are cushioned from shock by the spinal disks. These disks contain a fluid which acts as a shock absorber and allows flexibility. The spinal column, on the average, is designed to support a total of 500 pounds. Exceeding this weight places severe compression stress on the disks and eventually causes lesions which allow the shock fluid to leak out. When this occurs, separation between the individual vertebrae is no longer maintained, allowing the vertebrae to make contact with spinal nerves and causing severe pain. Once a spinal disk has lost its fluid, it cannot be replaced. Recurrent, severe pain is inevitable.

If you take a 10-pound weight and place it at the end of a 10-foot pole and attempt to lift it, it is as if you are lifting a 100-pound weight. The same ratio occurs when you bend at the waist and lift an object without bending your knees. The object places ten times its own weight in stress on your spinal column.

As stated above, your spinal column is designed to handle approximately 500 pounds of weight. The upper part of the body, including the head and shoulders, weighs on the average approximately 50 pounds. When a person bends over at the waist and comes back up to a vertical position, he or she is placing approximately 500 pounds of stress on the spinal column before lifting an object. Therefore, any amount of weight lifted without bending the knees and keeping the

Exhibit 4-10

back straight is exceeding the spinal column's load-bearing capacity. Eventually constant excess load will lead to injury.

Always bend your knees, keep your back as straight as possible, and lift with your legs.

The second most frequent cause of back injury is muscle strain, and this is most frequently the result of not warming up before attempting to lift an object. Muscle strain is also often caused by twisting the back as the result of keeping the feet stationary while turning with a load.

When cold, muscle fibers are very brittle and can tear easily. When warm, muscle fibers are very flexible and stretchable. Therefore, always warm up before lifting or performing any task that requires muscular flexibility. This can best be done by wearing the appropriate clothing for the temperature in which you will be working. Layers of clothing are preferable to one heavy garment.

Doing light calisthenics before beginning work each day and again after lunch, or any time your muscles have cooled down, can be very helpful in avoiding strain injuries.

Strained muscles are often a cumulative type of injury. Individual fibers that make up the muscle tear little by little over a period of time due to improper lifting technique or improper warmup. Then one day a strain is felt and presumed to have been caused by the work at hand, but actually this is seldom the case.

Always remember to step with the load. Never keep your feet stationary and twist with the load. This too is a major cause of muscle strain injuries.

Always use equipment, or get help when lifting any object which is too heavy for you to lift easily, or too bulky and awkward to lift.

Remember the rules for keeping your back healthy:

1.   Always bend your knees and lift with your legs.
2.   Warm up before lifting or doing manual labor.
3.   Never twist with a load, always step.

Exhibit 4-10 (*cont.*)

Finally, remember that you are responsible for your health and well-being. The life of an unhealthy or injured person is an unhappy one. Take care of yourself. Be concerned for your health. Eat properly and regularly. Eat good, healthy food. Avoid excessive sugar, salt, and highly processed food. Get sufficient rest at night. Allow time for daily exercise above and beyond the exercise you may get at work. Keep your muscles fit and toned. Your work will be easier and you will enjoy a long, healthy, and happy life.

Additional comments:

Attended by:

Exhibit 4-10 (*cont.*)

SAFETY MEETING REPORT

Date:
Conducted by:
Topic: The need to wear hearing protection

Hearing protection is required whenever the environment sound level exceeds 85db in the area where an employee is working.

Hearing protection is suggested and highly recommended whenever noise levels are above normal conversational volumn.

The company will provide you with one set of soft ear plugs, and one pair of ear muffs for those working in areas where ear muffs are required. This safety equipment will be assigned to you, and it is your responsibility to keep your equipment clean, and not lose it.

When it becomes worn from use, the equipment will be replaced free of charge. However, if you lose the set that is assigned to you or it becomes damaged due to negligence, you will be charged for the replacement set. Failure to maintain your safety equipment properly, and to wear it where it is required, will be noted on your personnel record and will be considered a violation of company safety policy.

It is very important to maintain your ear plugs with daily soap and water washing. The ear plugs should always be clean before they are inserted into your ears. At the end of each day it is best to wash the soft ear plugs in soap and water. Then dry them thoroughly with paper towels and place them in their protective case. This procedure is extremely important to avoid ear infection. (If you have been issued disposable ear plugs, please disregard the above.)

Ear muffs should be wiped clean with a damp towel and then dried as frequently as necessary to avoid deterioration. This should be done at least once a week.

Disposable ear plugs may be worn only for one day. They must be discarded at the end of each working day.

Exhibit 4-11

Hearing is accomplished by the bones that surround the ear as well as the ear itself. Sound entering the ear canal is transferred to auditory nerves by what is commonly known as the eardrum. The eardrum is vibrated by external sound that enters the ear through the ear canal. Excessive noise levels will cause the eardrum to vibrate excessively. Over a period of time, this will cause the eardrum to thicken and be less able to transfer the auditory impulses.

Beyond the eardrum are auditory nerves that relay sound impulses directly to the brain. The sensitivity of the auditory nerves is controlled by neurochemicals released by the brain in response to external sound levels. Excessive external sound levels will eventually cause a permanent reduction in the volume response of these auditory nerves. This reduction is gradual, insidious, and irreversible.

Auditory problems can also be caused by ear infection. Therefore, it is important to wear hearing protection in those areas where it is required and to keep your hearing protection equipment clean and sanitary.

In addition to the physiological damage created by excessive external sound levels, there is a significant increase in the fatigue created while working. Working without hearing protection in a noisy area is more tiring than working with the appropriate protection.

Fatigue is one of the major causes of accidents. Therefore, to reduce the chance of an accident, and to protect one of your most valuable senses:
ALWAYS WEAR HEARING PROTECTION WHEN IT
IS REQUIRED

Additional comments:

Attended by:

Exhibit 4-11 (*cont.*)

SAFETY MEETING REPORT

Date:
Conducted by:
Topic: Confined space entry

Note: Confined space entry is a complicated subject that requires careful training of all personnel involved. It is not the intent of this meeting to substitute for proper employee training.

A confined space is any enviroment or area which restricts the flow of pure air to the employee either by the physical configuration of the space, or by the patterns of air flow within the space.

Confined space atmosphere must be tested to ensure that the air within is safe to breathe. Always treat confined space as hazardous until the atmosphere has been tested by a qualified person. Further, confined space air should be monitored throughout the operation to ensure that the air within is fresh and safe to breathe.

Never allow yourself to be caught off guard. Rust, prior combustion, even bateriological action can reduce the oxygen content of the air below safe standards. Some gases are combustible, unbreathable, and odorless. Some can adversely affect your sense of smell, rendering it unreliable in warning of toxic atmosphere. Additional gases can be released as you are working.

Never enter a confined space without knowing the present state of the enviroment and what was contained in the confined space prior to your entry. Always lock out and/or tag any valves, switches, doors, or other possible entry points of substances while you are within the confined space.

Additional topics:

Attended by:

Exhibit 4-12

SAFETY MEETING REPORT

Date:

Conducted by:

Topic: Hard hats

The human skull is one of the hardest structures in the human body, but it is not impervious to injury.

A sharp edge of a beam or other protruding object can lacerate the skull and cause profuse bleeding.

A small and relatively light object falling 4 or more feet will have an impact force 4 times its resting weight, sufficient in many cases to penetrate the skull and causing death or serious concussion injury at the least.

Statistics indicate that more construction workers are killed each year by falling objects than by any other single event.

Wear your hard hat whenever you are in an area where there is a chance that you might be struck by a falling object or swinging tool, or might bump your head on a protruding object. Always wear your hard hat when working in or passing through areas where overhead work is being performed.

Your hard hat helps to disperse the energy of the blow over a greater area of your skull, absorb the shock of the blow, and deflect the direction of the blow.

Never store objects in the space between the liner of the hard hat and the outer shell. This air space contributes significantly to the energy-absorbing qualities of the hard hat. Reducing the air space can virtually eliminate the protective qualities of the hard hat.

Additional topics:

Attended by:

Exhibit 4-13

SAFETY MEETING REPORT

Date:

Conducted by:

Topic: Accident response preparation

Accidents will occur in spite of your best efforts. Injured people will receive first aid or some type of initial treatment from co-workers. Be prepared.

It is important to know how to respond to an emergency involving an injury. This will require that each person improve and maintain first aid skills.

Know where the first aid kit is located and how to use the supplies it contains. Know what medical facility will be called in case of a serious injury and how to communicate with that facility. This is especially important at remote jobsites and requires significant planning.

When an injury occurs, there is no time to read a book on what to do, so plan ahead.

1. Stay calm; do not allow your sympathetic emotions toward the injured party to get in the way of the action you must take.
2. Stop severe bleeding if at all possible, preferably with a tight compress.
3. Keep the victim lying down. Keep the victim covered to conserve heat and reduce shock.
4. If at all possible, stay with the victim and have another person call for help. If you are alone, call for help as soon as possible after applying compresses and/or covering the victim.
5. Never move the victim unless it is absolutely necessary, or give the person liquids or food.
6. Stay with the victim giving support and comfort until help arrives.

Additional comments:

Attended by:

Exhibit 4-14

SAFETY MEETING REPORT

Date:
Conducted by:
Topic: Falling objects

Falling objects are responsible for at least 10 percent of all reported injuries.

Most injuries caused by falling objects are caused by other people working overhead. Always wear your hard hat when you are in an area where overhead work is being performed.

Never throw objects from a height unless you are absolutely certain the area below is clear. This will require another person to stand below, well clear of the space where the object will be dropped, to ensure no other people inadvertently wander into the drop zone.

Always "flag off" under the area where you are performing work that involves the possibility of your dropping tools or other objects.

Take only the materials and tools necessary for the job you are performing. Use a pouch to transport tools up a ladder so that both hands are free to climb with; use a hand line to haul up tools too large for the pouch.

Place tools and material used above carefully to ensure that they will not be bumped off while you are working. Brace the tools and materials to ensure that they do not slide off or are blown off by the wind.

Avoid being the cause of a falling object injury. You could be held personally and in some cases criminally liable. Work safely and think of the safety of others as you are working.

Additional comments:

Attended by:

Exhibit 4-15

SAFETY MEETING REPORT

Date:
Conducted by:
Topic: Near accidents

Near accidents are as serious as injury accidents. They are a warning that someone was not operating in a safe manner. They may be considered "good luck" by the person nearly injured, but in fact are a harbinger of injuries to come. Every near accident is an indication that someone is not maintaining a safety-conscious attitude.

Near accidents should be reported to your supervisor and analyzed to determine the cause. Corrective action should be taken to avoid a recurrence.

Never use defective or damaged tools and equipment. Check your tools and equipment at the start of each work day, or before performing any operation with the equipment. Note any problems and have them repaired before beginning work. Even something as simple as a broken step on a dirt loader can lead to an injury because drivers will forget the step is broken when they climb down for lunch. Fix it first, then use it.

For every 10 near accidents, there will be 3 minor injuries and 1 serious injury. Elimination of near accidents will virtually ensure an injury-free operation.

Additional comments:

Attended by:

Exhibit 4-16

SAFETY MEETING REPORT

Date:
Conducted by:
Topic: The new employee

The new employee has the greatest chance of being injured because he or she is not used to the rhythm of the operation.

If the new employee is performing an operation which is new to him or her, the risk of injury is at least twenty times greater than that for an experienced employee.

Watch out for new employees. Be prepared to advise them if they are performing or about to perform an operation in an unsafe manner.

Always inform the supervisor of your observations and suggestions. This is not "finking" on the new employee. The supervisor is interested in the safety and well-being of the employees. In order to design an appropriate training program, the supervisor needs to know how the new employee is performing. The supervisor cannot watch the new employee at all times.

Remember that the new employee will look to the more experienced employee for clues on how to perform operations. Always set a good example by following safe operating procedures. Many new employees have been injured as the result of performing operations unsafely because they observed a more experienced employee performing those operations in an unsafe manner. Whether you realize it or not, you are setting an example for the new employee throughout the work day. Make certain the example being set is a safe one.

Additional comments:

Attended by:

Exhibit 4-17

SAFETY MEETING REPORT

Date:
Conducted by:
Topic: Recurring accidents

Each year millions of people are injured in industrial accidents. Sadly, these accidents are too often recurrences of accidents that have happened before in the same operation.

Nearly all accidents are preventable. Nearly all accidents occur because an employee failed to follow safe operating procedures.

Approximately 2,500 construction workers die in work-related accidents each year, accidents that for the most part were completely avoidable. To avoid accidents, safe operating procedures must be followed at all times. Resist the desire to "save time" by taking a shortcut.

Always take the time to analyze near accidents and then take the steps necessary to avoid a recurrence. Remember, a near accident is an injury in the future if corrective action is not taken.

Many injuries occur each year to employees going to the aid of an injured co-worker. When an emergency occurs, the desire to help the injured person often overrides normal caution. Don't become an additional victim. Take time to analyze the situation and determine the safest way to effect the rescue. Becoming a victim while attempting a rescue will be of no benefit to the originally injured employee. You cannot help someone if you are injured yourself in the process.

Additional comments:

Attended by:

Exhibit 4-18

SAFETY MEETING REPORT

Date:
Conducted by:
Topic: Road work

Maintaining roads and bridges employs many people. Unfortunately, many people are also injured while working on our national road network.

Road work involves the use of heavy equipment including loaders, graders, cranes, and trucks of all types. Stay alert. Be aware of what is going on around you. Remember the environment around heavy equipment is noisy. It is easy to become used to the noise and begin to ignore it. When this occurs, the employee is in danger of being run over.

Never allow employees to work under suspended loads.

Working on traveled highways is always hazardous. Each year hundreds of workers are struck by vehicles traveling along highways where road work is being performed. Flag-persons must be alert for the oncoming driver who is not paying attention.

Always follow safe operating procedures when erecting or maintaining bridges. Use appropriate safety equipment, including safety belts, hard hats, lanyards, and other equipment to protect the employee from falling. Unfortunately, many of our nation's bridge caissons and concrete work are tombs and silent monuments to workers who have fallen into the concrete while building the structure.

Additional comments:

Attended by:

Exhibit 4-19

SAFETY MEETING REPORT

Date:

Conducted by:

Topic: Trench work

Every year, approximately 150 employees die from excavation cave-ins. Nearly every death was preventable.

Always follow safe operating procedures as prescribed by OSHA standards. Proper sloping, shoring, and/or use of a "shield" should be in place before any worker enters a trench or excavated area where a cave-in or slide is possible.

Never assume the ground is safe. Minor earth tremors can cause the collapse of an apparently solid wall of dirt. These earth tremors occur throughout the world every day, not just in places famous for earthquakes. The ground is an excellent transmitter of sound and vibration. A heavy truck going along a highway within one mile of an excavation site can in some instances be sufficient to cause a cave-in.

When working in a trench in association with a back hoe, stay well clear of the bucket's maximum reach and radius of operation. Regardless of the skill of the operator, a hydraulic line failure can cause a bucket to drop instantly.

Never work in a trench when a loader is scraping and removing dirt, rock, or concrete alongside the trench.

Additional comments:

Attended by:

Exhibit 4-20

SAFETY MEETING REPORT

Date:
Conducted by:
Topic: Shoring

Never guess at shoring requirements. Always consult an expert when choosing material for shoring. Shoring requirements involve many factors other than the mechanical knowledge of how to construct a temporary wall. Load-bearing capacity and soil conditions must be accurately estimated. Strength under all weather conditions and the stresses imposed during various phases of construction must be taken into consideration.

The length of the trench of the slope being shored has a significant bearing on the strength of the shoring wall. Generally, the longer the wall, the less bearing capacity it will have.

When installing manufactured shoring, never take short-cuts. Follow installation instructions exactly. Use all pins, clamps, braces, and other accessories called for in the instructions. Always inventory parts before and after using shoring material to ensure that the next job will have all the necessary parts. "For want of a nail, a life was lost."

Additional comments:

Attended by:

Exhibit 4-21

SAFETY MEETING REPORT

Date:
Conducted by:
Topic: Air-powered tools

Air-powered tools are driven by compressed air delivered from portable compressors, or permanently located compressors in manufacturing enviroments.

Compressed air when used improperly can cause serious injury. Never use compressed air to hose yourself off, or to hose off another person.

If compressed air is being used to blow chips from working surfaces, safety goggles must be worn by all persons within the immediate area. Never intentionally blow chips in the direction of yourself or another person.

In plants where oxygen and other flammable gases are used, hoses and delivery pipes must be properly labeled and color-coded. Always identify the air or gas pipe before hooking up a delivery hose.

Oxygen can spontaneously ignite in the presence of lubricant oil. Never attach a powered tool to an oxygen line. Make certain that delivery hose connections used for oxygen and oxygen/gas combinations are kept very clean. Even a small amount of oil can cause a spontaneous flash fire at the connection.

Always depressurize delivery lines before connecting or disconnecting tools and equipment.

When using grinders, carefully monitor the speed of the tool. Air pressure can fluctuate, causing the tool to overspeed. This can lead to spontaneous disintegration of the grinding wheel. The effect is similar to that of a hand grenade.

Never point pneumatic tools at another person. If the retainer device fails, the tool can fire a deadly projectile.

Always safety-chain hose connections together to avoid whipping injury should the hose disconnect under pressure.

Attended by:

Exhibit 4-22

SAFETY MEETING REPORT

Date:
Conducted by:
Topic: Conveyor systems

Material conveyor systems are becoming more and more common in many types of working environments, including manufacturing, food service, and construction.

Material conveyor systems are driven by chains, belts, screw shafts, air, and vacumn systems. Each drive system presents unique hazards.

Never attempt to unjam or perform maintenance on a conveyor system without first shutting off, locking out, and tagging the system controls.

During conveyor operations, be alert for materials which might fall from overhead due to jamming or other malfunction. Never remove drive guards or attempt to unjam a conveyor system while it is in operation.

Never use a conveyor system as transportation from one point to another. Never walk on drive system guards or covers. These can collapse, allowing the worker to fall into the drive system.

Always wear safety goggles and respirators around air and vacuum-driven conveyor systems due to the level of airborne particles generated by these types of systems.

Be very careful of all pinch points, sprockets, gears, belts, and any moving parts. Never wear loose clothing, or allow long hair to hang about the neck and shoulders. Clothing and hair can be grabbed by moving parts, causing serious injury.

Additional comments:

Attended by:

Exhibit 4-23

SAFETY MEETING REPORT

Date:
Conducted by:
Topic: Heating systems

All heating systems that use a flame to deliver heat can deplete usable oxygen in a confined space. As oxygen is depleted, unburned fuel may begin to enter the enviroment. This combination is deadly.

Always ensure that there is proper ventilation whenever a flame-powered heater is in use. Never close or seal off a space, even a relatively large space. Given sufficient time, any space will become oxygen-deficient without adequate ventilation.

All liquid- and gas-fueled heaters must have a safety control to ensure that fuel delivery will cease should the flame be inadvertently extinguished.

Never use open-flame heaters in an area where fuel, gasoline, or other flammable vaporizing liquids are stored. Vaporizing liquids can travel just above ground level to flame sources due to convection currents created by heat rising and cold air flowing along ground surfaces. This can lead to sudden and disastrous explosions. Make certain there are no pathways for vaporizing liquids to follow to a flame heater source.

Many office and line assembly workers use portable electric heaters to warm the immediate workspace. Always make certain that manufacturer's directions are followed in regard to placement distance from the worker. Electric heaters can gradually raise skin surface temperatures, causing severe cumulative burns, without the worker being aware of the injury developing.

Exhibit 4-24

Never use electric coil heaters in areas where flammable vapors may be present. Minute sparks or coil electrical shorts can ignite flammable vapors. Always make certain all electrical cords are in good condition and do not create trip and fall hazards.

Additional comments:

Attended by:

Exhibit 4-24 (*cont.*)

SAFETY MEETING REPORT

Date:

Conducted by:

Topic: Fire prevention

Each year, nearly 800,000 residential and 50,000 industrial fires do serious damage to people and structures. Yet very few workers ever stop to consider the importance of fire prevention. They assume that someone else is responsible for their safety.

All workers must accept the responsibility of fire prevention. This means eliminating the sources of combustion by maintaining good housekeeping, cleaning up scrap, and proper storage of flammables.

Never overload electrical circuits, outlets, fixtures, or cords. Do not use extension cords in the presence of moisture that can lead to short circuits. Make certain all electrical circuits conform to code. Electrical fires can smoulder in woodwork, walls, and roofs for hours or days and suddenly burst into an uncontrollable and deadly conflagration.

Every worker needs to know and have in mind a fire escape plan from any portion of a structure. Never work in a structure without having first learned the fastest and safest method of egress in the event of a fire.

At home, make certain you have a working smoke detector. Check the batteries regularly. Have a fire extinguisher handy in the kitchen, garage, and near the fireplace. Make certain you and your family have agreed on a plan of escape and a place of meeting. Never reenter a burning building for possessions left behind. Fire will use up oxygen very quickly, and smoke is deadly. More people die from smoke inhalation and lack of oxygen in fires than from the flames themselves.

Exhibit 4-25

When using a fire extinguisher, never direct the propellant at the center of the flames. This will spread the fire. Always attack the fire at the edge, using a sweeping action to extinguish the fire away from you.

Additional comments:

Attended by:

Exhibit 4-25 (*cont.*)

SAFETY MEETING REPORT

Date:
Conducted by:
Topic: Lift platforms

Never attempt to operate a lift platform without appropriate training. Every worker must be trained and signed off by a supervisor prior to operating a lift platform.

It is very important to remain alert to what is going on around a lift platform operation. Due to the reduced speed of hydraulic operations, it is very difficult to descend quickly to escape a developing problem.

Make certain the lift unit is stable and the wheels cannot move before ascending. Always wear a safety lanyard which is appropriately attached to the lift platform, as recommended by the manufacturer. Never attach a safety lanyard to adjacent structures.

Never use a lifting platform as a crane. Tools, equipment, and people should only be lifted in the approved manner. Never exceed the rated load capacity. Repeated lifting of excessive loads will lead to metal fatigue and collapse. Lifting platforms should be X-rayed for metal fatigue at least annually, or as recommended by the manufacturer. Always perform a thorough equipment safety check before ascending on the platform.

Never use ladders on the lifting platform to extend the height. Stay at least 20 feet from all power lines. Do not ascend in a platform in winds exceeding 25 miles per hour. Be especially cautious when winds are gusting.

Never move from one point to another with the aerial platform extended. Such movement significantly increases the chance of tipover due to the increased "arm moment" to weight ratio. A small bump or wind gust can be deadly.

Additional comments:

Attended by:

Exhibit 4-26

SAFETY MEETING REPORT

Date:
Conducted by:
Topic: Electrical shocks

The leading cause of death in crane operations is electrical shock from making contact with high-voltage wires. Never allow yourself or your equipment to come into contact with overhead electrical wires.

The most common electrical voltages encountered by workers are 110 and 220. 110 volts is generally thought to be nonlethal, but this is not the case at all. Each year hundreds of deaths occur as the result of contact with 110 volts of electricity.

Electric shock causes paralysis of the muscles due to an overloading of the nerve fibers with electrical potential. If this occurs in the chest area, the heart muscle can cease to function and death will occur.

The chance of death or serious injury is greatly increased by the presence of moisture. Standing on a damp surface while experiencing an electrical shock will triple the chance of serious injury or death.

Always make certain that all tools and equipment are properly grounded, and that extension cords are well insulated, without nicks or frays in the insulation. Never use three-prong plugs in two-prong receptacles. Always use three-prong fully grounded connections. Protect lightbulbs from breakage. Use ground fault circuitry on all construction sites.

Use insulated tools when working with wiring. Tag and lock out circuit breaker panels when working on wiring. Keep the work area free of water and conducting debris.

Additional comments:

Attended by:

Exhibit 4-27

SAFETY MEETING REPORT

Date:
Conducted by:
Topic: Burns

Many burn hazards exist within the work environment. Here are a few tips:

Never wear oil- or gasoline-soaked clothing. The slightest spark can ignite the cloth, and the substances alone can cause severe cumulative skin irritation.

Never use oxygen to blow dust off skin, clothing, or work surfaces. Oxygen will spontaneously combust in the presence of lubricants. Oxygen molecules can adhere to fabric and combust hours later in the presence of a spark, flame, or lubricants.

Never refuel vehicles or equipment while they are operating, or if hot parts are in close proximity to the fuel. Never smoke around refueling equipment.

Use caution around hot equipment. Hot parts can cause severe burns. Never open a radiator cap if the radiator, hose, or engine is warm to the touch. External parts will cool rapidly at low temperature, leaving the internal fluid under pressure scaldingly hot. Never lean directly over a radiator cap when removing it. Wear heat-resistant gloves and protective clothing when removing a radiator cap if there is any chance that the coolant is still hot.

If clothing catches fire, immediately drop to the ground and roll.

Treat minor burns with cold water or intermittent short-term ice application. Do not attempt to treat serious burns. Call for medical attention immediately. Cover the burns with dry sterile dressings. Be prepared to treat the victim for shock.

Additional comments:

Attended by:

Exhibit 4-28

5

CENTRALIZED HIRING

Careful selection of employees cannot be overemphasized. Employees with preexisting injuries or a proclivity toward work-related injury are very likely to incur injuries again while working for a new employer. The ability to recognize a good potential employee from a group of candidates is both a learned skill and an intuitive talent. However, regardless of how talented a manager may be at choosing productive, safe employees, intuition must be backed up by corroborative reference check information.

CHECKING REFERENCES

Every employee, regardless of the position to be filled, responsibility attendant on the position, or wages earned, should be reference-checked prior to being offered the position. Many employers will reference-check employees being hired for positions of responsibility and/or high wages but neglect to reference-check the minimum-wage, low-responsibility applicant. This approach represents a clear misunderstanding on the part of the employer of the effectiveness of reference checks as a loss control tool.

It is the low-wage earner with the least responsibility who

can most easily live on the benefits provided under compensation law. A person assuming greater responsibility, with the attendant higher wage, is far more interested in returning to work as soon as possible. Therefore, failure to perform reference checks on all candidates is simply reducing, or perhaps completely negating, the value of performing any reference checks at all.

Laws and regulations of the Equal Employment Opportunities Commission, Labor Department and/or other related state and federal watchdog agencies associated with hiring practices stress the need to disclose to all candidates the employer's intention to conduct reference checks, and the need to maintain nondiscriminatory consistency in implementing the reference-check policy.

An employer who checks only some employees is running a greater risk in regard to discriminatory practices than an employer who performs checks on all candidates. The reasoning here is obvious. If the employer hires one candidate without a reference check while denying employment to another after a reference check, there is an inconsistent policy that implies discriminatory practices.

Many employers avoid conducting any preemployment reference checks because they are under the impression that such checks are not allowed under EEOC regulations. This is not the case at all. Employers are constrained from providing confidential data to future employers. And future employers are constrained from using confidential data as a basis for deciding to hire a candidate. However, an employer may ask any question that relates directly to the job requirements of the work the candidate will be doing for the employer. This simple test will warn any employer away from discriminatory questions: *If the question does not apply directly to the job requirement of the work the candidate will be doing, it should not be asked.* For example: An employer is hiring an employee to perform a job that requires repeated bending and lifting. Which of the following questions may be asked during a reference check?

- *What is the religious affiliation of the employee candidate?* No. It has no bearing on the duties to be performed.
- *To your knowledge, has the candidate ever suffered a back injury?* Yes. The job requires repeated bending and lifting. A prior

back injury should be taken into consideration. The labor code requires that no employee be placed in a position where work he or she is performing would endanger them or other workers. A person with a preexisting back injury may be endangered by work requiring repeated bending and lifting.

Can a candidate be refused employment based upon a positive answer to this question? No, but the employer then has the right to ask the candidate for permission to contact the treating physician for an opinion of the candidate's ability to perform the task for which he or she would be hired. If the physician feels that such work would be likely to aggravate the preexisting condition, then the employment may be denied on that basis alone. If the treating physician is not available or the injury occurred in the distant past, the employer may require the candidate to pass a preemployment medical examination at the employer's expense. The employer may choose the physician.

- *Has the employee candidate ever suffered a work-related injury?* Yes.
- *Has the candidate ever collected workers' compensation benefits?* No. The fact that a candidate has collected compensation benefits does not relate directly to the work the candidate will be performing. Furthermore, the employer is concerned about preexisting injuries that may adversely affect the candidate's ability to perform the work of the job. Such preexisting conditions may occur outside the work environment and not be covered by compensation benefits.

The important point to remember is that EEOC regulations do not exclude any questions from preemployment screening as long as they relate directly to the intended work duties. In our example, the first question was not allowable because it had no relationship to the duties in question. However, if a church or religious organization were hiring a minister, then reference-check questions concerning religious affiliation would be justifiable.

Employers are sometimes discouraged from conducting preemployment reference checks because in the past they were unable to gather any information from previous employers due to the previous employers' lack of understanding or fear of discriminatory lawsuits. Nevertheless, the effort must always be made. Preemployment screening is too important to ignore. At the very least, answers to the following questions can be obtained:

- Verification of employment.
- Verification of duties.
- Verification of salary.
- Is the candidate eligible for rehire?
- If No to above: Is it a policy not to rehire former employees?

Answers to the last two questions will provide some insight into the quality of the candidate under consideration.

Many employers make the mistake of assuming that all former employers listed on an employment application in fact represent "all" the former employers. In some cases, candidates may wish to exclude employers with whom they have had unhappy experiences and so will simply leave them off the application. While this fact may be brought to light through a discrepancy in employment dates as shown on the application versus results on reference checks, it is always good to elicit from the former employer the name of the previous employer as shown on its records. This prior employer should also be contacted, because information from this new source may prove crucial to the hiring decision. Exhibit 5-1 shows a typical application form.

Once a decision to hire or not to hire is made, the candidate should be informed. However, information gained from former employers should never be divulged to an applicant unless such information is requested in writing by the applicant.

There are really only two reasons why an applicant is not hired: (1) The job did not become available as anticipated. (2) The employer elected to hire someone else whom he felt was better qualified. Voluntarily sharing reference-check data with applicants is foolish, as it can lead to serious problems for former employers and for the present employer.

APPLICATION FOR EMPLOYMENT

Applicants are considered for all positions without regard to race, color, religion, sex, national origin, age, marital or veteran status, or the presence of a non-job-related medical condition or handicap.

(PLEASE PRINT)

Date of Application _____

Position(s) Applied For _____

Applicant Profile

Name _____
 LAST   FIRST   MIDDLE

Address _____
 NUMBER   STREET   CITY   STATE   ZIP CODE

Telephone (_____) ____ Social Security Number ____|____|____
 Area Code

If employed and you are under 18,
can you furnish a work permit?   ☐ Yes ☐ No

Have you filed an application here before? ☐Yes ☐No If Yes, give date _____

Have you ever been employed here before? ☐Yes ☐No If Yes, give date _____

Are you employed now? ☐Yes ☐No
May we contact your present employer? ☐Yes ☐No

Are you prevented from lawfully becoming employed
in this country because of Visa or Immigration Status? ☐ Yes ☐ No
(Proof of citizenship or immigration status may be required upon employment.)

On what date would you be available for work? _____

Are you available to work ☐Full Time ☐Part-Time ☐Shift Work ☐Temporary

Are you on a lay-off and subject to recall? ☐ Yes ☐ No

Can you travel if a job requires it? ☐ Yes ☐ No

Have you been convicted of a felony within the last 7 years? ☐ No ☐ Yes

If Yes, please explain _____

Exhibit 5-1

APPLICATION FOR EMPLOYMENT *(cont'd)*

Veteran of the U.S. military service? ____ Yes ____ No

If Yes, Branch _____

Do you have any physical, mental or medical impairment or disablity that would limit your job performance for the position for which you are applying?
____ Yes ____ No

If Yes, please explain _____

List professional, trade, business, or civic activities and offices held. (Exclude those which indicate race, color, religion, sex or national origin): _____

_____

_____

Give name, address and telephone number of three references who are not related to you and are not previous employers.

_____

_____

_____

SPECIAL EMPLOYMENT NOTICE TO DISABLED VETERANS, VIETNAM ERA VETERANS, AND INDIVIDUALS WITH PHYSICAL OR MENTAL HANDICAPS.

Government contractors are subject to Section 402 of the Vietnam Era Veterans Readjustment Act of 1974 which requires that they take affirmative action to employ and advance in employment qualified disabled veterans and veterans of the Vietnam Era, and Section 503 of the Rehabilitation Act of 1973, as amended, which requires government contractors to take affirmative action to employ and advance in employment qualified handicapped individuals.

If you are a disabled veteran, or have a physical or mental handicap, you are invited to volunteer this information. The purpose is to provide information regarding proper placement and appropriate accommodation to enable you to perform the job in a proper and safe manner. This information will be treated as confidential. Failure to provide this information will not jeopardize or adversely affect any consideration you may receive for employment.

If you wish to be identified, please sign below.

____ Handicapped   ____ Disabled Veteran   ____ Vietnam Era Veteran

Signed _____

Exhibit 5-1 *(cont.)*

APPLICATION FOR EMPLOYMENT *(cont'd)*

Employment Experience

Start with your present or last job. Include military service assignments and volunteer activities. Exclude organization names which indicate race, color, religion, sex or national origin.

1) Employer	Dates Employed		Work Performed
	From	To	
Address	Hourly Rate/Salary		
	Starting	Final	
Phone No.			
Job Title			
Supervisor	Reason for Leaving		
2) Employer	Dates Employed		Work Performed
	From	To	
Address	Hourly Rate/Salary		
	Starting	Final	
Phone No.			
Job Title			
Supervisor	Reason for Leaving		

Exhibit 5-1 *(cont.)*

APPLICATION FOR EMPLOYMENT *(cont'd)*

3) Employer	Dates Employed		Work Performed
	From	To	
Address	Hourly Rate/Salary		
	Starting	Final	
Phone No.			
Job Title			
Supervisor	Reason for Leaving		

4) Employer	Dates Employed		Work Performed
	From	To	
Address	Hourly Rate/Salary		
	Starting	Final	
Phone No.			
Job Title			
Supervisor	Reason for Leaving		

Exhibit 5-1 *(cont.)*

APPLICATION FOR EMPLOYMENT *(cont'd)*

Education

	Elementary	High	College/University	Graduate/ Professional
School Name				
Years Completed: (Circle)	4 5 6 7 8	9 10 11 12	1 2 3 4	1 2 3 4
Diploma/Degree				
Describe Course Of Study:				
Describe Specialized Training, Apprenticeship, Skills, and Extra-Curricular Activities				

Honors Received _____

State any additional information you feel may be helpful to us in considering your application. _____

_____

Exhibit 5-1 *(cont.)*

AGREEMENT

I certify that the answers given herin are true and complete to the best of my knowledge.

I authorize investigation of all statements contained in this application for employment as may be necessary in arriving at an employment decision. I understand that this application is not intended to be a contract of employment.

In the event of employment, I understand that false or misleading information given by me in this application or in interviews may result in discharge. I understand, also, that I am required to abide by all rules and regulations of the Company.

Medical history, physical examination, and drug screening test are a requirement for employment with the Company.

_____   _____
Signature of Applicant   Date

AN EQUAL OPPORTUNITY EMPLOYER M/F/V/H

Exhibit 5-1 (*cont.*)

Negative reference-check information should be corroborated by a pattern of prior employment behavior. Any former employer who is too willing to divulge negative information should be suspect in regard to the valididty of such information. Normally, negative information must be drawn out of a former employer. A question that may be effective in this case is: We all have our strengths and weaknesses; in which areas do you feel the candidate could improve his or her work habits?

All reference-check information is highly confidential and should be handled, whenever possible, by only one experienced and trusted company employee. Never allow this information to circulate among other company employees. Allowing such a practice will generate an indefensible position in regard to privacy laws and/or discriminatory practices.

In Summary

Contact all former employers on all candidate positions. Verify all application information given, and continuity of employment. Be wary of volunteered negative information. Keep all reference checks confidential.

6

DESIGNATED PHYSICIANS AND MEDICAL FACILITIES

An important feature of an effective loss control program is the development of a designated physician/medical facility program. Many employers shy away from having such a program because they do not wish to infringe upon employees' freedom to choose their own physicians for treatment of a work-related illness or injury. In fact, labor and worker compensation laws do not allow an employer to infringe upon such freedom of choice. However, effective claims management depends upon the employer having some degree of knowledge and control of where an employee will go to seek medical attention. Furthermore, employers are required to have designated medical facilities to treat emergency injuries in the most expedient manner, including transport to such a facility when an injury occurs. This information must be posted and be readily available to all employees, not just supervisory or management personel. Workers' compensation law requires that the name and address of the employer's workers' compensation insurance carrier be posted as well. Normally all this information is contained on one emergency poster which is posted in various strategic areas throughout the operation.

THE PROGRAM

The designated physician/medical facility program consists of three levels: facility, physician, chiropractor.

Designation of an Emergency Medical Treatment Facility or Facilities

An employer is required to establish a procedure for dealing with an injured employee under emergency circumstances. Such a procedure must include designation of the facility to which the injured employee will be transported, designation of the method of transportation, and posting of the names and telephone numbers of those to be contacted in the event of an emergency.

Emergency walk-in clinics are excellent choices as a designated medical facility when the clinics are in close proximity to the employer's location. These clinics are less expensive than hospital emergency rooms and very effective for dealing with common minor injuries in the workplace. However, for life-threatening or very serious work-related illness or injury, a fully staffed hospital must also be designated. It is best to choose a hospital with which your designated physician is familiar.

Designation of a Physician

Having a physician with whom the employer has established a working rapport is perhaps the best defense against employees who attempt to work the system and malinger with questionable symptoms.

Designation of a Chiropractor

Many employers feel that all chiropractors are quacks and abhor the idea of actually designating such a practitioner. Nevertheless, many employees will seek chiropractic treatment and may actually benefit from such treatment. Under labor and workers' compensation law, such treatment is considered legitimate. Since there is nothing an employer can do to prevent an employee from seeking such treatment, it is best to choose the chiropractor to have a degree of control over the duration of treatment.

Unfortunately, the abuses perpetrated by some in the chiropractic profession have led many employers to distrust all chiropractors. Some chiropractors will extend treatment beyond that which is really beneficial to the employee in order to improve their personal income profile. When the occasional walk-in patient is covered under workers' compensation insurance, this provides an excellent opportunity for the unethical chiropractor to take advantage of the system.

When an employer chooses a chiropractor there is an opportunity to designate one with a good reputation and an ethical standard of operation. This standard, of course, is reinforced by the fact that the designated chiropractor can expect to receive numerous industrial patients over a period of time, eliminating the incentive to take advantage of the occasional walk-in situation.

In fact, chiropractors can be an employer's first line of defense in recognizing the employee who is just looking for some time off. In many instances, their skilled manipulation of extremities and pressure points can reveal more about the true condition of the patient in regard to perceived pain than the most advanced electronic imaging devices presently available to orthopedic physicians.

ESTABLISHING A SUCCESSFUL PROGRAM

In order to establish an effective designated medical facility program, these steps must be followed:

1. Locate the nearest emergency medical facility(ies).
2. Visit the facility and talk with the administrator to determine its ability to handle the types of emergencies most likely to occur with your employees.
3. Talk to other employers in your area to determine what results they may have had in using the facility.
4. Develop referrals on both physicians and chiropractors from other employers in your area. Interview these individuals.

5. When you have chosen the facility(ies), physician, and chiropractor, inform your employees using a form similar to the sample in Exhibit 6-1. Have employees sign an individual form agreeing to go to your designated facility(ies), physician, or chiropractor. Place the signed form in their personnel file.

    Employees, by law, may choose their own physician, chiropractor, or medical facility at any time prior to a work-related injury or illness. However, if they do not so choose before the event takes place, they are obligated to go to the designated physician for at least 30 days. Thereafter, they may choose a physician of their own if they are not satisfied with the treatment they have received. A sample form for an employee's designated physician is also included in this chapter (Exhibit 6-2).

6. Arrange to have the designated physician, facility(ies), or chiropractor contact you immediately if an employee comes in for a work-related illness or injury. Also arrange to have all bills sent to you for forwarding to your insurance carrier. This can best be accomplished by explaining to the facility that the fastest way to get paid is to send you the bill so that you may send it to the appropriate person at your insurance carrier's office for prompt payment.

Receiving the billings directly gives you the most complete control of the treatment process. If the treatment appears inappropiate or overextended, you may request your insurance carrier to seek a second opinion. Remember, never choose a second opinion yourself without your insurance carrier's approval. If a second opinion corroborates the first treating physician's diagnosis and treatment, you are stuck with those conclusions. Let your carrier help you with questionable situations, as it will most likely have had experience with the physicians in question.

There have been many instances where employees have been released to return to work and employers have assumed the treatment had been terminated, only to find out that it had not been when the insurance carrier's loss run reflected the costs involved. Always have your insurance clerk follow up on

NOTICE OF WORKER'S
COMPENSATION BENEFITS

For purposes of on-the-job injuries and diseases:
(*Name of employer*) is insured for Worker's Compensation by (*name and address of insurance company*). However, if you suffer an on-the-job injury or illness, you should report it immediately to your supervisor or a management person of your employer.

If you suffer an on-the-job injury or illness, you will be entitled to all medical treatment with an employer-designated physician reasonably required to cure or relieve you of the effects of the injury or illness. If, after thirty (30) days from the date of injury or onset of illness you still require medical treatment, you will have the opportunity of selecting a physician of your choice.

If you have designated, on a form available to you, a physician as your "personal doctor" prior to suffering an on-the-job injury or illness, you may be treated by that physician within the first thirty (30) days from the date of injury or onset of disease.

You may also be entitled to temporary disability indemnity payments for those periods of time during which you are unable to work due to the effects of the on-the-job injury or illness. You or your dependents may also be entitled to permanent disability indemnity, vocational rehabilitative services, where appropriate, and dependency benefits in cases of death.

(*Name of employer's physician*)

I have read and understand the above.

Signature _____ Date _____

Exhibit 6-1

EMPLOYEE DESIGNATION OF
PERSONAL PHYSICIAN

In the event that the undersigned employee of (*name of employer*) should suffer an on-the-job injury or illness, the undersigned designates (*name and address of physician*) as their personal physician with whom they select to undertake treatment for such injury or disease. The undersigned employee represents that (*name of physician*) is the employee's physician who has previously directed their medical treatment and who retains their medical records, including their medical history.

Signature _____ Date _____

Exhibit 6-2

employee treatment even when you are supposedly receiving all billings. This follow-up should include determining if treatment is ongoing, an estimate of termination, and an estimate of costs. Medical facilities tend to close cases more expediently when they know the employer is keeping an eye on the progress of the employee.

EMPLOYER-PAID FIRST AID PROGRAMS

Many employers prefer to pay for the small, unavoidable first aid claims that occur rather than send these claims to an insurance carrier. In most states, this practice is not allowed by labor law or the insurance code because it destabilizes the rating formulas which are designed to set fair experience modifiers for all employers, reagardless of the size of the employer's workforce. Frequency of injury is a valuable component of these formulas, and nonreporting of minor first aid claims can upset the integrity of the modifying formula.

However, in some localities payment of small first aid claims is allowed. Before embarking on the following program, consult your state's Department of Insurance in regard to the legality of instituting an employer-paid first aid program. The program begins with an effective designated physician program, as described above. However, those claims which fall into the category of first aid as defined by your state's labor code may be paid by the employer rather than reported and forwarded to the insurance carrier.

An insurance carrier is obligated under Department of Insurance regulations to establish a reserve on all claims reported to its claims department for payment. If the reserve is not closed out prior to unit statistical reporting to the state's rating authority, the incurred expense used in the unit stat report will include both the actual amount paid for the "first aid" claim and the reserve established. This reported cost is much higher than the actual amount paid alone and consequently adversely affects the rating of the claim for experience modifier purposes.

It is for this reason that many employers prefer to pay the "first aid" claim themselves, when legally allowed to do so, rather than report the claim to an insurance carrier. If such a policy is allowed and elected, it is crucial that the employer make the decision in regard to payment within 5 working days of the date of injury, or the date the employee first reported the injury or illness. Most insurance carriers and state law require industrial injuries to be reported within 5 working days. In order to meet these stringent time requirements, an effective accident investigation procedure must be in place, along with an effective designated physician program.

To make the appropriate decision, the employer's insurance clerk will call the treating physician for a definition of treatment, diagnosis, and prognosis. The clerk will then receive an estimate of cost from the treating facility and make a decision whether or not the claim will fit into the employer-paid first aid program. If so, the employer pays the medical bill when it arrives. If not, the insurance carrier's first report of injury form is completed and sent to the carrier, along with all appropriate accident investigation documentation within the 5 working day period. The medical bills are then forwarded for payment as they arrive.

It is important that employers always complete the insurance carrier's first report of injury form regardless of whether or not the injury meets the criteria of a paid first aid program. Occasionally a "first aid" injury will become more complicated and will need to be turned into the carrier. Having the first report form already completed will simplify and expedite the process.

Remember the criteria of decision between a reportable claim and an employer-paid first aid claim is not the dollar amount charged for treatment, but rather the definition of the treatment needed for any given event. The employer always has the option of sending the claim to the insurance carrier should the dollar amount exceed the limit for cost of employer-paid first aid.

7

TRAINING

OSHA Safety Orders require that all employers provide initial training and necessary recurrent training for employees. Lack of training and supervision is one of the most common causes of serious employee injury. Often employees are injured because they have not followed the proper work procedure. An employee performing a task incorrectly is an injury waiting to occur. Given sufficient time, it will occur.

- It is not sufficient that the employer be able to prove that training was made available; the employer must be able to prove that the employee received the training and became qualified to perform the task for which the training was required.
- Training requirements are not limited to large employers: *all* employers must provide employee training.
- Training is not limited to complicated work, or hazardous machinery or operations. Employers must be able to show that an employee has demonstrated the ability to safely perform the work they have been assigned.

Supervision of employees to ensure that work is being performed in the approved way is paramount in successful training. Employees will often know how to accomplish work in an unapproved manner and fall back into "old habits" after being taught how to perform the work in the approved way. This is normal. The trainer should anticipate that the employee will return to previous methods of operation after initial training, particularly if a "rush" situation comes along.

LEARNING NEW WAYS

All people find new operations difficult when compared to the "old" way. This is due to the way in which the brain remembers task performance. The brain develops memory pathways which are linked in overlapping patterns. The *engrams,* or memory patterns, which allow a person to select a fork and use it to place food into the mouth have many identical components to the engrams that allow a person to select a spoon, or use fingers to put the food into the mouth. This interface of related memories conserves the brain's energy in processing data. And once an engram is established, it is virtually impossible to erase.

Since many procedures will use common memory pathways, new training procedures will be interwoven into common components of old methodology. Unfortunately, the old, unrelated components have established a "deeper" pathway that causes the brain naturally to seek the prior, less resistant course. This fact translates into extra mental effort in order for the employee to conform to the new procedure.

If a rush production schedule intervenes during establishment of new engrams, or if fatigue reduces the mental energy available, the employee will automatically return to the former operating procedure. And if the former procedure is hazardous and the employee is mentally and/or physically fatigued, or his or her concentration is interrupted, an accident will ocurr.

Psychologists have determined that the fastest way to establish new brain patterns or work habits is to train employees in the following manner:

1. Break tasks down into their basic components. No training step should contain more than one operational component. *Example:* It would be inappropriate to include activating a

machine guard in the same training step as activating the operation of the machine.

2. Verbally explain how and why the step is to be followed. *Example:* The machine guard is lowered into place to protect you from the possibility of making contact with the cutting edge of the die. This guard contains a safety interlock that will not allow the machine to operate if the guard is not in proper position.

3. Demonstrate how the task is to be performed.

4. Ask the employee to explain the procedure. Ask the employee to explain why the procedure is necessary. If either explanation is incorrect, return to step 2.

5. Have the employee demonstrate the procedure.

REVIEW

When operating procedures involve several steps, and especially when the steps are relatively complicated, it is necessary to review the prior steps at two or more places in the training process. Normally, a review is conducted halfway through the task training process and again two thirds of the way through the process. This review should include an explanation and demonstration of all prior steps by both trainer and trainee.

When the training process is complete, the employee should be assigned a low workload with no time constraints for completion of the work. The trainer should observe the employee's performance to ensure that all steps are being followed correctly. During this time, the trainer may need to demonstrate some or all of the steps involved again.

When the trainer is confident that the trainee is capable of performing the task safely, the trainer leaves the trainee to do the task on his or her own for a short period of time. After the time has elapsed, the trainer should return and again observe the employee at work. The return should be timed to coincide with the end of the task. Trainers must make their presence known before the trainee begins a repeat operation. The trainer should, prior to returning for the first operational review following the trainee's solo activity, observe the trainee's performance at a distance without the trainee's knowledge of this observation. Never interrupt a trainee's task performance, even if it is incorrect, unless the trainee is in imminent danger of injury to himself or another worker.

During review sessions, the trainee should always compliment the trainee on those portions of the task properly completed, while again explaining and demonstrating the portions that have not yet been properly learned. Some tasks will require no more than two reviews; other tasks or individuals may require many. The trainer must be a patient individual.

Some trainees feel extreme stress while learning new tasks, even tasks that may seem very simple to the trainer or other trainees. This adverse stress level may be attributed to a lack of confidence on the part of the trainees in their ability to perform a new task correctly. This lack of confidence can often be traced to memory patterns developed at a very young age as the result of physical or verbal insults by adults, siblings, or peers, especially when combined with physical or mental impairments beyond the control or perceived control of the young trainee. These memory patterns are virtually unforgettable and are restimulated every time the trainee must face a new task. The more complex the task, the stronger the restimulating effect.

The trainer may overcome the effect of such stress by frequent positive reinforcement of the trainee's ability to accomplish the new task and by referring to the progress made, regardless of the time required. Occasionally a trainer will encounter individuals whose adverse training memories are so strong they are unable to learn the task correctly regardless of the amount of training. Often these individuals want to learn the task and may, in fact, have gone to great lengths to gain the opportunity to learn the task. The trainer must establish reasonable parameters of learning with some degree of flexibility to account for the variety of trainees. Nevertheless, the trainer must understand that some individuals are untrainable due to lack of inherent talent or past adverse memory patterns.

It is not the role of the trainer to determine the root cause of a trainee's inability to learn a task correctly. If the trainer is unable to train the employee to perform the task safely, the trainee must be moved to another position or terminated. *Allowing any employee to perform a task incorrectly will lead to an injury.*

Each of us has adverse training memories, but some people have more adverse patterns than others. The trainer must learn to recognize from body language, tone of voice, and confidence of action those trainees who have had past negative training memories stimulated. Some trainees will cover up stress feelings with bravado or apparent confidence. This is easily recognizable. A trainee who is covering up lack of confidence will not be able to explain why a step must be performed, even though he or she may be able to perform the step correctly. It is extremely important that a trainer never allow a trainee to perform a task solo without being able to explain why each step in the task is necessary.

The "Sign Off"

When a trainee has demonstrated the ability to perform the task correctly, has received two successful review sessions with at least 48 hours between the first and second review session, he or she may be signed off to perform the task as a regular employee. But the trainer's responsibility does not end with the initial "sign off." Recurrent reviews must be done at increasing intervals until the trainer is positive that a complete memory pattern has been established. This can be determined when all of the following factors coincide:

- Task is performed correctly at each observation.
- Production is at acceptable levels.
- Employee smiles broadly or laughs aloud when the trainer says: "Well, do you feel like you own this (machine, tool, name of job, task)?

Trainers should be aware that all trainees will have inconsistent learning curves, with plateaus and even setbacks. This is normal and to be expected. In fact, the trainee who does not experience a temporary learning plateau during complicated training procedures may not have completely grasped the material at all. Trainees who seem to learn the fastest are often those most in need of more frequent recurrent training.

NEW EXPERIENCED EMPLOYEES

Employers frequently hire employees to perform work for which they appear to have prior experience. The fact that candidates indicate verbally or in writing their ability to perform work does not in any way guarantee that they can perform the work safely, to the employer's standards. All new hires should be required to demonstrate their ability to perform the work for which they have been hired, or may be expected to perform in the future. The employer should:

- Separate the new employees' work into individual units.
- Ask the employees how they will perform each individual unit.
- If the explanation appears to fit within the parameters of the employer's procedures, ask the employees to demonstrate the work.
- If the employees successfully demonstrate the work, they may be signed off to perform the duties for which they were hired.
- If the employees cannot demonstrate the work to the satisfaction of the employer, they must be trained.

Employees who have performed work for other employers successfully but who do not meet the standards of the new employer are normally resistant to training. This fact must be taken into consideration by the trainer, but should have no bearing on the employer's decision to train.

Occasionally, employees will refuse to perform a task as an employer requires because they feel their old method of operation is safer. In most cases they are wrong, but in some cases they are right. The employer should give the new employees an opportunity to explain why the old method is safer. Their explanation should be given due consideration. Sometimes a combination of a new employee's method and the employer's method creates an even safer procedure. However, the employer must take into consideration how the procedure will fit into the total safety picture for the operation. If employer and employee cannot agree, it may be necessary to terminate the new employee in order to maintain the integrity of the operation. For this reason, a 90-day training/probationary period is valuable.

TRAINING DOCUMENTATION: CHECKLISTS

As with other aspects of a loss control program, all training should be documented. Many employers fail to document training efforts because they are not prepared to write a complete training manual. But this is not necessary; in fact, under some circumstances it can negate the value of training documentation. Having too much detail associated with documentation can create a situation where an attorney seeking benefits for an employee uses a training manual to prove that significant gaps existed in the training procedures which ultimately led to the alleged or actual injury.

Training and related documentation needs to be flexible enough to take into consideration the wide variety of learning curves for employees taking such training. The best way to provide flexibility and reduce the sheer volume of training documentation is through the use of training checklists.

The checklist acts as a reminder to the trainer to cover the essential points involved in the training while allowing an opportunity for adjustment to the level of the trainee. As each point on the checklist is covered, the trainer initials its completion. When the employee is completely trained, both trainer and employee sign the checklist and indicate that the training is complete. The signed checklist should then be placed in the employee's personnel file for future reference. Space should be provided on the checklist to allow the trainer to add additional points which may be covered as experience develops with a particular operation, or if additional emphasis is needed for a particular trainee.

A checklist can be developed by using these steps:

1. Begin the process with the end result of any procedure or machine operation. Work backward from that end point, noting each stage of the operation or procedure performed by the employee. Write each of these stages down.
2. Assign a number to each stage, from the beginning to the end. These are the training checkpoints.
3. Observe an employee during the operation and confirm each checkpoint. Continue to observe the operation, noting all precautions taken at each checkpoint and all hazards associated with each checkpoint. These become subpoints which must be covered. Often a checkpoint will be benign in regard to hazards, but critical to the final end product. Checkpoints may have subpoints associated with hazards, with critical end point procedures, or both. However, subpoints should be limited to no more than four. If more

than four subpoints are identified, the trainer should establish another checkpoint.

4. The training checklist should have no more than twelve
    checkpoints, each with a maximum of four subpoints.
    Occasionally, an operation will require a longer checklist.
5. Trainers often combine an unjamming, emergency, or
    maintenance checklist with a standard operational checklist.
    This is a serious mistake. Emergency procedures, un-
    jamming, or maintenance checklists should always be
    separate. Furthermore, these checklists should be used for
    recurrent training on a regular basis.

Checklists are critical and must be drilled and reviewed to
ensure that the employee will react in the appropriate manner
when required. An example of what can happen is shown in
Exhibit 7-1.

The operational checklist can be developed in this way.

Work backward, and identify each stage of the operation:

- Helper sorts and stacks.
- Helper removes trays and scrap.
- Helper depresses "start" buttons on his side of machine.
- Operator depresses "start" buttons on his side of machine.
- Operator loads machine.
- Operator selects sheet of trays from stack.

Assign numbers and work forward:

1. Operator removes sheet from stack.
2. Operator loads machine
3. Operator observes helper to be in position to press "start"
    button. Operator and helper may exchange glances or
    words to delineate readiness to activate machine.
4. Operator and helper press start buttons. Press comes down
    rapidly, cutting trays.
5. Helper removes trays and scrap.
6. Operator gets another sheet and loads machine.
7. Helper sorts and stacks trays.

Operation: Power press, die cutting machine. Employee removes a sheet of vacuum-formed food trays from a stack, loads the sheet into the power press, and activates the machine by pressing start buttons. The press comes down rapidly, trimming the sheet around the trays with a die. A second employee removes the cut trays and the trimmed plastic, stacks the trays, and discards obvious rejects while the operator is loading the next sheet.

Maintenance operations include: removing a die when dull, and replacing it with a substitute and sending the first die to the machine shop for sharpening. Jamming may occur when plastic trim gets wedged into the die after a cut is made.

Accidents have included: A helper being cut when the die slipped from the upper press during a change of dies and fell onto the helper's hand.

Corrective action: Both operator and helper wear leather gloves when removing the die.

Accident: An operator once lost four fingers when a helper reenergized a machine while the operator had his hands under the press after replacing a die. The press had moved down during shutoff, and the operator had made a motion which was interpreted by the helper to mean "cycle the machine." The operator had not followed proper procedures. The machine was not "de-energized and locked out"; a "creep" block was not in place to prevent the press from creeping down; the operator did not discuss the procedure with the helper; and no clear signals or words were used to identify required actions.

Exhibit 7-1

Some operations still use power presses that have only operator buttons. Helper is supposed to signal when clear. Operator is not to depress the start button until helper indicates he is clear. Any employer with a similar operation is strongly urged to add two additional start buttons for the helper so that the machine cannot be operated unless all four buttons are depressed at the same time. No amount of training will prevent a helper accident without four start buttons—it is only a matter of time.

Next, observe the operation to ensure that all checkpoint stages are covered, then add subpoints:

1. Must lift trays by edges to avoid denting.
2. Operator must use care to avoid cutting knuckles on die. Must make certain trays are flush to mold's surface.
3. Operator nods to helper and says "Ready"? Receives acknowledgment and activates machine.
4. None required.
5. Helper must use extra care when removing scrap to avoid cutting fingers on die. Gloves are not feasible due to bulk.
6. None required.
7. None required.

The result is an operational checklist like that in Exhibit 7-2.

The emergency procedures/maintenance checklist is developed through the same steps. However, unlike the training checklist, it is used on a regular basis for drill and recurrent training (Exhibit 7-3).

When doing recurrent training it is not necessary to have the employee actually perform every step in the operation. However the employee(s) should describe exactly how the operation is to be performed, point to the appropriate switches, and identify and handle the lock-out tag and creep block. Frequency of recurrent training depends upon the experience of the employees involved and the success of the prior training session. In any case, recurrent training should be carried out no less the twice a year.

FINAL OPERATIONAL CHECKLIST

1. Operator removes sheet of trays from stack.
   A. Extra care must be used to avoid denting trays.
2. Operator loads trays onto mold.
   A. Care must be used to avoid cutting knuckles on die.
   B. Care must be used to make certain trays are flush and even on mold.
3. Operator asks helper if he is ready. Receives acknowledgment.
   A. The use of the word "Ready?" is encouraged.
4. Operator and helper depress their Start buttons.
5. Helper removes cut trays and scrap.
   A. Must use care to avoid cuts from die.
6. Operator selects another sheet and loads machine.
7. Helper sorts and stacks while operator is setting up next cut.

Additional comments:

Trainer _____   Date _____

Trainee _____

Exhibit 7-2

MAINTENANCE CHECKLIST

When trays are being cut unevenly or incompletely:

1. Shut off machine at circuit breaker located on the left side of the machine (from the operator's point of view).
2. Close lock-out cover and tag with lock-out tag.
3. Place creep block under press.
4. Loosen hold-down bolts on die.
5. Operator and helper must put on gloves prior to removing hold-down bolts.
6. Operator removes hold-down bolts. Helper supports die.
7. Remove die and replace with new die.
8. Helper takes old die to machine shop. Operator checks bolts and die position.
9. Operator removes creep block and places test tray into machine, then allows press to creep to the full down position.
10. Operator removes lock-out tag. Each lock-out tag has the name of an operator on it. Only the operator named may remove the lock-out tag.
11. Operator energizes machine by moving circuit breaker to On position, after ensuring that helper's hands are clear.
12. Operator and helper depress Start buttons and cycle the machine.

Trainer _____ Date _____

Trainee _____

Exhibit 7-3

TRAINING DATA SOURCES

Where machinery and equipment is concerned, the employer may look to the manufacturer and/or distributor for training material and aids. Manufacturers normally develop operation manuals and in some cases training films, slides, or self-teaching courses for their equipment. These sources are not a substitute for one-on-one training, nor are they a replacement for the training checklist. The sources are very good for developing the training checklist and delineating the checkpoints of primary importance. Nevertheless, operation of the equipment in the employer's environment will necessarily require designing the training course to fit actual on-site conditions.

SUPERVISION VS. TRAINING

Very often the trainees' supervisor will also be their trainer. This may be the most expedient and practical approach, given the experience of the supervisor and budgetary constraints. However, supervisors must differentiate between day-to-day supervision and training.

The employee must realize that training is something that requires concentration, be it initial or recurrent training. The checklist is valuable, because it specifies points to be covered, shows the complete operation, and requires the signature of the trainee and trainer upon completion. This creates a much more "important" atmosphere in the mind of the trainee, which enhances the training effect.

Supervisors often make the mistake of thinking that daily operational reminders can replace recurrent training. This is not the case at all; such thinking inevitably leads to accidents. When the accident investigation is conducted, the supervisor invariably says: "I reminded the employee several times not to do that." This is a perfectly true statement in many cases, and absolutely worthless in preventing the injury. Repeated admonishments by a supervisor to an employee to follow a specific procedure, or to watch out for a specific hazard, indicate the need for training.

The successful learning of a skill, or the following of an appropriate procedure, involves the complete understanding of the purpose of the procedure and the reason for the sequence of steps in the operation. If an employee is skipping a step, it is because he or she does not fully understand the reason for the procedure. Of course, some employees simply do not have the capacity to learn and need to be rotated out of the position before they injure themselves or co-workers. However, this decision cannot be made fairly without a thorough training program and good documentation of training efforts.

Some employers make the mistake of thinking that safety meetings and safety inspections, with counseling of employees, are substitutes for training. Again, as with supervision, these techniques do not replace the need for initial and recurrent training. Yet both procedures are important and valuable in an employer's loss control efforts. Training is vital to the success of any loss control program. It must be well thought out, consistently provided, and well documented. The time and effort spent on training will prove most profitable to the overall efficiency and success of any business operation.

8

ACCIDENT
INVESTIGATION

An accident investigation should be conducted whenever an accident or a near accident occurs. Very few employers realize the value of conducting an accident investigation when a near accident occurs. In fact, less than 5 percent of all employers follow this important procedure. Yet an investigation conducted following a near accident is perhaps the purest form of loss control, because corrective action taken at that point may prevent an actual future injury. The near accident investigation is not as time-consuming as an accident investigation completed following an injury. Witness and claimant statements are normally not necessary. Corrective action may be as time-consuming as would be the case following an injury, but well worth the time invested, as a future injury is avoided.

Employers wise enough to conduct near accident investigations and take corrective action should certainly maintain documentation of the investigation and the corrective action. This type of loss control will prove very beneficial to an employer's case should it ever become necessary to defend the employer's loss control efforts in a court of law.

In this chapter, we concentrate on the steps involved in conducting an accident investigation following a serious injury accident, or the reporting of a questionable claim. An accident investigation is paramount in identifying a condition that needs correction, and is also the primary tool in the management of questionable or fraudulent claims. Employers who routinely conduct thorough accident investigations have a far lower incidence of questionable claims, as well as a lower incidence of serious accidents.

Accident investigation is an art which must be learned over time. The more practice an employer has at the process, the better the corrective action taken and the more successful the loss control program. This presents a paradox, because the more effective the loss control, the fewer the accidents that occur, and the fewer opportunities to practice accident investigation techniques. Practice in the form of near accident investigation is the solution.

CONDUCTING THE INITIAL INVESTIGATION

The initial accident investigation should be conducted by the injured employee's supervisor. This individual is most familiar with the operation being performed by the injured worker, and usually most familiar with an injured worker himself or herself. The accident investigation completed by the supervisor should be reviewed thoroughly by the safety director and additional detail added as needed. The safety director is responsible for obtaining all claimant and witness statements.

When an accident occurs, the first priority is to get medical treatment for the injured employee. As soon thereafter as possible, the accident investigation should be conducted. Time is of the essense for two reasons: (1) the environmental conditions that existed at the time of the accident will change, and (2) the opinions and perceptions of the injured party and of witnesses will change.

Typically, an injured worker goes through the following psychological stages after an injury:

• The initial reaction is one of embarrassment. The only thought is to get well and get back to work. At this first stage, the injured party normally believes that he or she has made some sort of error and is responsible for the injury.
• If the injury is very serious, shock will set in.

- As the shock wears off and the employee comes to the realization that he or she is not going to recover immediately, the person will begin to analyze the accident. Depending on the severity of the injury, the analysis will take place within 2 hours of the accident. It is critical that an interview with the employee be conducted from 1 to 3 hours following the injury if at all possible. If 8 or more hours elapse, the employee's perceptions of the events will have been significantly altered by rationalizations.
- Within 24 hours following the accident, the employee will have come to the conclusion that something or someone (the employer) is responsible for the injury, even if in fact the employee made a significant contribution to the injury.
- If the injury is permanent, the employee will blame the employer entirely. This feeling of blame may take several weeks to set in, but it inevitably will occur.

Whether or not the employee attempts legal action against the employer will depend primarily upon two conditions: (1) the severity of the injury and (2) the employer/employee relationship preceding and succeeding the accident. Good faith, concern, and sincere interest in helping an employee following an accident can go a long way to mitigating the blame the employee feels toward the employer.

The employer must realize that regardless of how much the employee has contributed to an accident, a degree of responsibility accrues to an employer either from the standpoint of training or of supervision. Many employers are unwilling to see that they play a role in an accident caused primarily by improper procedures being followed by the injured employee. The unwillingness of the employer to accept a degree of responsibility may eliminate the ability to correct the circumstances that led to the accident in the first place. A recurrence is therefore likely, if not at the same work station, then in another situation where training or supervision is less than sufficient. Unfortunately, to one degree or another, we all learn only from our mistakes. If we are unable or unwilling to face this fact of life, we simply do not learn at all and set the stage for the unproductive repetition of prior errors.

The fact that we learn only from mistakes is so obvious that most people do not realize the significance of this old adage. There is no situation where new knowledge is acquired that does not result in some initial error of performance that requires an operational adjustment. Let me repeat that statement: *There is no situation where new knowledge is acquired that does not result in some initial error of performance that requires an operational adjustment.* Most of us call this adjustment *experience.* Every accident or near accident investigation presents an opportunity for an employer to make the necessary operational adjustment to reduce the chances of a recurrence. However, this opportunity can be taken advantage of only if the employer is willing to: (1) recognize its responsibility and contribution to any accident and (2) take the necessary corrective action.

However, we need to differentiate between legal admission of responsibility and philosophical admission. No employer should be foolish enough to publicly—verbally or in writing—state that it is responsible or partially responsible for an injury. Legal responsibility is best reserved for the insurance carriers and courts to decide. Yet philosophically each employer must have an attitude that any accident, regardless of severity, is unacceptable and that it is the responsibility of the employer to eliminate the conditions that lead to employee injury.

CASE STUDY: AN ACCIDENT INVESTIGATION WHERE SERIOUS INJURY IS INVOLVED

The injured employee's supervisor conducts the initial investigation.

1. After providing first aid treatment and having the employee transported to the hospital, the very first step is to take photographs of the accident location, including the equipment involved and the surrounding area. The photographs should be taken from all perspectives. Never include other employees in the photographs, and never take photographs of the injured party(ies). Do not alter the scene in any way. Take the photographs exactly as the area appears immediately following first aid treatment and transportation of the injured person to the hospital. Use a 35-millimeter single-lens reflex camera with built-in flash, or an autofocus 35-millimeter camera with built-in flash. Use 400 speed color negative film for the photos.

Every employer should have such photographic equipment on site and available for the safety director to use.

2. Using an accident investigation form, the injured employee's supervisor begins the investigation process. The use of such a form helps to focus the attention of the investigator on the questions that need to be answered. Everyone, no matter how experienced, suffers a degree of shock following an accident, especially if they are involved in the treatment of an injured person. Using a form with the appropriate questions (Exhibit 8-1) helps the investigator to overcome the initial shock.

Form Questions and Their Significance

A typical form will begin with preliminary questions concerning the following: company, department, duties; name of injured (social security number and age of the injured employee can be filled in by the safety director); occupation, length of employment (can also be filled in at a later time).

Date of Accident? Hour of Occurrence? These questions are important from a statistical standpoint, and may also have some bearing on determining the cause(s) of the accident. For instance, some injuries have occurred just at coffee break time, when an employee was distracted or rushed as the result of hearing the chime from a mobile canteen truck. The hour of the accident and the events taking place at the time the injury occurred may be pertinent to future corrective action.

On Employer's Premises? Address? These are questions primarily for statistical purposes, but are important basic information as well. Subsequent court and/or insurance case documents may contain the wrong address and location of an injury. Such basic information may prove very important to the final adjudication of the case.

Describe the Injury/Illness. It is very important for the supervisor to describe in his or her own words the injury observed sustained by the employee. Detail is important.

SUPERVISOR'S REPORT OF ACCIDENT

Company: _____ Dept. or Job: _____

Name of Injured:_____Soc. Sec. No.:_____ Age: ___

Occupation (Title): _____ How long employed: _____

Date of Accident:_____Hour:_____at Employer's Premises Yes☐ No☐

Address Accident Occurred: _____

Name of Physician: _____ Hospital: _____

Describe injury/illness (be specific) _____

_____

_____

What was injured doing _____

_____

_____

How did injury/illness occur (what went wrong) _____

_____

_____

_____

Remedy to prevent similar accidents _____

_____

_____

Action taken to prevent similar accidents _____

_____

_____

In your opinion, is this a valid claim? Yes ☐ No ☐ If no, explain ___

_____

Date:_____Supervisor's Signature_____Supervisor's Title____

(USE OTHER SIDE AS NEEDED)

Exhibit 8-1

What Was the Injured Employee Doing? The supervisor should indicate the operation the employee was performing, including the steps he was following to complete the operation prior to the injury.

How Did the Injury Occur? This form question is very important, and really includes the question, Why did the injury occur? The space provided on the form for this and the following questions is insufficient for accurate detail. Additional paper should be used as needed to answer the remainder of the questions completely.

Remedy to Prevent Similar Accidents? This is undoubtedly the most important question on the form, and the whole reason for conducting the accident investigation.

Action Taken to Prevent Similar Accidents? This question is not normally answered by the supervisor during the initial investigation, but filled in by the safety director following completion of the full investigation and implementation of corrective action. Unfortunately, many safety directors fail to complete this one detail even though corrective action is actually implemented. Too often the accident investigation form has been used by the insurance clerk to fill in the first report of injury and then filed with a copy of the insurance form. *It is very important that this question is answered and documented in detail.* This documentation will have a significant effect on the rulings of a judge and/or jury should the matter end up in court.

Review of prior accident investigations and corrective action taken is a routine part of any OSHA inspection or insurance underwriting survey. Employers who do not appear to take corrective action create a very adverse image for themselves in the eyes of those who will pass judgment on the sincerity of their loss control and safety efforts.

In Your Opinion, Is This a Valid Claim? If the answer is no, explain. Dealing with the questionable or invalid claim will be discussed later in the chapter. It is enough here to say that if the supervisor or safety director feels that the claim is invalid, a detailed explanation should be made here.

Application of Investigative Techniques to the Case Study

[*Note:* Only first names are used for this example. All names and locations are fictitious. Any similarity to names, places, people, and events is purely coincidental.]

The injured employee was operating a table saw. Guarding of the saw blade was not possible due to the type of wood being cut. The employee was required to repeatedly make cuts of wood used in other phases of the operation. His only job, 8 hours a day, was to cut 1" × 8" × 36" boards lengthwise into 1" × 2" × 36" strips. The procedure followed was to place a 1" × 8" board on the table and push it through the saw. After the cut was made, the 1" × 2" strip was removed and placed on a stack, which was subsequently removed for production by a helper. The employee used a wooden "push stick" for all cuts.

The accident occurred when the employee was making a third cut. The employee's right hand, which was used to push the wood through the blade, made contact with the blade. The little finger, three-fourth of the third finger, and one-half of the middle finger below the middle finger joint were amputated.

His cries of pain brought immediate assistance from both his supervisor and another employee who had some first aid training. The hand was immediately wrapped in sterile bandage from the first aid kit. The severed fingers were placed in ice available by chance from another employee's ice chest, and an ambulance was called to transport the injured employee to the hospital.

[This is a true accident. The employee permanently lost the fifth and third fingers. The middle finger was reattached and 80 percent use was regained after two years of treatment. The employee was placed in a rehabilitation program and trained to drive a truck. Total cost of medical treatment and rehabilitation: $103,000. Total time from injury to reemployment: 3 1/2 years. The employee sued employer for serious and willful violation of OSHA regulations—failure to train properly and failure to guard equipment. The employer lost the lawsuit due to prima faciae evidence provided by an OSHA citation and a subsequent recurrence of digital amputation on another power saw. The employer, as the result of punitive damages awards assessed on both accidents, was forced into bankruptcy and is now out of business. Failure to investigate the accidents properly and take appropriate corrective action was the cause of the employer's bankruptcy.

Therefore, the following investigation and corrective action is hypothetical. Nevertheless, the steps and techniques discussed will provide an example of the elements involved in investigating any serious injury accident.]

After the injury described above and transportation of the injured party to the hospital, the following accident investigation takes place:

Fred, the shift supervisor, returns to the scene of the injury with the company safety director. Production has come to a halt, and some workers have asked to go home. Two of these workers witnessed the accident. They are asked by Fred to wait in his office to be interviewed. Fred is very sympathetic to their feelings, but asks for their cooperation because he wants to determine the cause of the accident and take whatever corrective action is necessary so it does not happen to anyone else.

One of the employees is willing to stay, but the other is a close friend of the injured employee. She is visibly upset and concerned about the injured employee. Fred indicates that he understands and asks if she has transportation. She says she does, and indicates that she wants to find out if Jim, the injured employee, is okay. Fred knows he cannot detain the witness involuntarily, or even use his authority to detain her. So he asks her if she is willing to come back later that afternoon to talk with him. She indicates that she will. Fred makes an appointment to see her at 4:30 and allows her to leave.

While this conversation is in progress, the safety director has cleared the area of bystanders, asking them to return to their workstations, where their supervisors will talk to them and assess if production in areas not related to the accident can continue. Unfortunately, the accident involved a key part of the production line, so it is decided to shut down the operation for the rest of the day. All production employees who were not witnesses to the accident are allowed to go home.

While this assessment is being made and before the decision to shut down is made, the safety director takes photographs of the accident scene. He uses a single-lens reflex camera with 400 color negative film. Although the camera has a built-in flash, it is not necessary to use the flash because of the fast film and adequate ambient lighting. This is good because it ensures that artificial shadows will not be created by the flash and reduces the employee distraction created by a flash going off while the safety director is photographing the accident scene.

The safety director is careful not to change anything associated with the accident scene. He photographs the area exactly as it appears. He cannot be sure that the scene has not been disturbed by other employees immediately following the accident or in the process of tending to the injured worker. However, at least from this point forward, the scene is uncontaminated.

The safety director first photographs the area from a perspective well behind the operator position. Next he shoots from the left and the right and finally from the front of the operator's position. The resulting photos give a good overall view of the area. Next the safety director moves in and photographs the machine from the operator's perspective and then to the left, right and front close in. The next few photographs detail various aspects of the scene and the machine involved in the accident. He photographs the push stick, the unfinished cut, and any other pertinent details. Altogether, he has taken 24 photographs. By the time the safety director has completed photographing the area, the decision to shut down production for the rest of the day has been made.

Inasmuch as Fred also witnessed the accident, he askes Fred to fill out the accident report form while he interviews the witness. The safety director asks the personnel manager to sit in on the interview. The witness is a woman, so the safety director has asked a woman to join him at the interview as his witness. An interview should involve the accident witness, the interviewer, and an interview witness who is of the same sex as the accident witness. This eliminates any future charge of intimidation or sexual harassment.

At the witness interview, the safety director explains to the witness that the purpose of the interview is to obtain the facts involved in the accident, not to place blame. He indicates that he is very sorry to see an employee injured and that the company wants to do whatever is necessary to prevent a recurrence. The first step is to find out what happened.

The safety director asks the witness to describe what she saw occur. He asks her to write in her own handwriting what she has just told him. He then asks her if she has any opinions or additional comments she would like to add. She indicates that she feels the employee was very tired from staying up late the night before and that he should not have been working today. The safety director asks the witness to add her comments to the notes she has written. However, she refuses because she does not really know that he was too tired to work. The safety director does not press the issue, but does ask her to sign and date her notes, which she does willingly. He asks her if she has transportation home. The witness indicates that she does not because the person she usually rides with has already left. The safety director then asks the personnel manager to arrange transportation for the witness. Immediately following the interview, the safety director makes notes of the impressions he has gained from the interview, including the additional comments made by the witness that were not included in her signed statement.

While this interview is taking place, Fred has been filling out the accident form.

> *Date/hour/place.* August 12, 1988—at approximately 2:15 P.M. in the production department.
>
> *Address.* 1555 South St., Beach, CA 00111
>
> *Name of Physician, Hospital. (left blank)*
>
> *Describe injury.* Employee lost three fingers while operating a radial table saw. He also may have suffered contusion to his lower back and side when he fell down after stumbling backward following the injury to his hand.
>
> *What was injured doing?* Jim was assigned to cut 1" × 8" by 3 foot lumber into 1" × 2" by 3 foot strips to be used as bracing for the subflooring of hot tubs. The process involves taking a piece of lumber from the stock stack, placing it on the table saw, and pushing it through the saw. A push stick is used to push the wood through the saw and keep the fingers away from the blade.
>
> *How did injury occur?* I am not sure exactly how the accident occurred. Jim is an experienced worker and always used the push stick. In fact, unlike most operators, he made a special push stick out of wood with a handle that kept his hand up

and away from the blade. This allowed him to push the wood all the way through the blade while keeping his hand well above and clear of the blade. Most operators just grab any old scrap and use it to push the wood through.

I can only think that maybe his hand slipped off the handle of his push stick and into the blade. When I asked him what happened after we gave him first aid, he said his hand just slipped into the saw.

Remedy to prevent similar accidents? I don't know except to be more careful. Jim was following the usual procedure.

Action taken to prevent similar accidents? (left blank)

In your opinion is this a valid claim? Yes

After Fred fills out the form, he brings it to the safety director's office, where they discuss the accident and the statement given by the witness. Fred is also quite upset, and the safety director suggests that he go home. Fred indicates that he has an appointment with the other witness at 4:30 P.M. However, the safety director does not expect the employee to keep the appointment and suggests that they will talk with her tomorrow. Fred checks with his superior, who agrees, and then goes home.

The safety director goes back to the scene of the accident and looks it over very carefully. The company president is also there. Together they look at the machine, surrounding scrap, stock, and completed work. The safety director picks up Jim's push stick. It has been cut in two by the blade severing the grip right where his fingers were holding it. He continues to look around and eventually finds the rest of the push stick, identifiable by the missing part of the grip.

The company president, who is an experienced wood worker, puts the two pieces together and examines them. He notes that the push stick looks like a science fiction weapon when held upside down and recalls seeing Jim walking around at break time with it stuck in his belt. When turned right side up, the handle rests on the pusher portion of the push stick and is used like a wood planing tool. The president notes that the pusher portion of the stick is now very narrow. He can tell by the portion attached to the handle that the pusher portion was much wider when the push stick was made. And therein lay the cause of the accident. Jim made a push stick which he felt was superior to using scrap. He was very proud of his creation and used it beyond the point of safety. Each time he pushed the wood through the saw, a very thin strip of the pusher was cut away. Eventually it became so narrow that it required care and concentration for Jim to push the wood he was cutting through the blade. He may have been tired, or bored, or distracted, but in any case he lost his concentration and his hand toppled over because the pusher portion of his push stick was too narrow. After examining the push stick, looking at the table saw in operation, and listening to the president's explanation, the safety director agreed completely with the president's analysis.

At this point many employers would stop the investigation because the primary cause of the injury has been determined. The primary cause was improper procedures—use of a custom-made pusher stick beyond the point of safe operation. The secondary cause was inadequate supervision. The supervisor should have noted the condition of the pusher stick and directed the employee to substitute a fresh one.

On the following day, the safety director and the personnel manager visited Jim at the hospital. They brought get well cards signed by other employees and showed concern for the comfort of the employee. Although Jim is being given prescription pain suppressors, the attending physician feels that he can answer a few questions coherently. Additionally, the injured employee has not as yet retained an attorney and is willing to answer questions about the accident.

Since Jim cannot write his own statement, the safety director has brought along a tape recorder. Jim has agreed to have the interview taped. A fresh tape is used and the recorder will not be turned off once it has been started, unless the interview is interrupted by medical personnel. If it is interrupted, the time, date, reason for interruption, and people present at the interview will be recorded on the tape. This information is again recorded at the next start of the tape. The tape will have no erasures. If a witness wishes to change a statement, he or she is allowed to do so by indicating a desire to correct a previous statement. The correction is then added. Erasures can be reason to disallow the tape as admissible evidence in court. At the beginning of the tape the witnesses should state their names and addresses and willingness to voluntarily give the statement.

The safety director asks Jim to describe what happened. His story centers on the fact that he was feeling pressed to complete a certain number of cuts in order to keep up with production. He feels that he was following proper procedures and using a pusher stick which he made and has always used. When asked if he feels the stick may have contributed to the accident, Jim indicates that he does not think so. He feels that the cause was too much pressure to complete the job. The safety director does not discuss the conclusions arrived at by the president and himself at this point in time. He is interested only in getting the injured employee's opinion of the accident. There will be plenty of time for training the employee in the proper procedures when he returns to work.

When Jim is asked what could be done to prevent a similar accident in the future, he indicates that he feels the job is too boring, leading to errors, and suggests that corrective action should include rotation of employees so that no one does the same repetitive job for the whole day. He also thinks that production time should be slowed down so that employees do not feel so pressed to complete work. The safety director thanks Jim for his statement and wishes him well. This is not the only time the safety director will visit Jim. However, all future visits will be informal "get well" visits. Some additional information may develop, but it will not change the outcome of the investigation.

When the safety director returns to work, he meets with Jim's supervisor. They discuss Jim's interview and also the conclusions reached the day before. The safety director does not blame the supervisor. He simply discusses the contributing factor of the custom pusher stick. However, the supervisor recognizes his role and volunteers that he should have realized what was going to happen. He justifies his decision to allow the use of the custom pusher stick because Jim seemed so proud of it and it was doing the job. The safety director simply indicates that it is a lesson to be remembered in the future.

At this point no corrective action has been suggested, even though a primary cause has been determined. However, the informal corrective action is to make certain a proper pusher stick is used by Jim's replacement. The safety director and Jim's supervisor then discuss the interview held with the other woman witness. No new information appeared other than the possibility that Jim may have been tired from having stayed out later than usual the night before. In the afternoon of the day following the accident, the safety director holds a general safety meeting with all the other employees. He indicates that Jim will be in the hospital for some time and that there is a good possibility that his fingers will be restored. He indicates that one of the causes of the accident was the fact that Jim allowed the pusher stick to get too thin, making it unstable, and he cautions all employees to use pusher sticks of the correct thickness.

The purpose of this initial safety meeting is to relieve the anxiety of the employees, to reduce rumors that will have circulated as to the cause of the accident, and to initiate immediate corrective action of the primary cause of the injury. However, complete corrective action will involve consideration of primary and secondary causes. Once complete corrective action has been decided on, policy and procedure will be established and communicated to the employees through their individual supervisors. To avoid unnecessary legal implications, full corrective action in regard to secondary causes is simply implemented as soon as possible. There is no need for discussion with all the other employees; only an initial general safety meeting is held in regard to the accident.

It takes the safety director approximately two weeks to develop the complete corrective action profile. The following is a summary of contributing factors and corrective action taken:

> *Primary cause:* Improper procedures—use of custom pusher stick beyond safe operation.
>
> *Secondary cause A:* Inadequate supervision—supervisor should have noted unsafe condition and taken immediate corrective action.
>
> *Secondary cause B:* A time and motion study reveals excessive time for one employee at repetitive, high-risk task. Employees are to be rotated between two or if possible three jobs to provide variety and reduce fatigue. This will also provide production flexibility. The Human Resources Department is to develop skill parameters for future new hires to ensure that all new hires can be rotated. Current employees are to be trained for rotation and terminated if unable to learn at least two repetitive tasks.

Custom-designed pusher sticks manufactured by employees are forbidden. Custom-designed pusher sticks have been ordered from a local metal fabrication shop. These consist of a metal plate to which is attached a wooden board that can be replaced as it is shaved off by the machine. Welded to the metal plate is a handle very similar to the one designed by Jim. Surrounding the handle to enclose the outside portion of the employee's hand exposed to the saw blade is a metal guard similar to that found on a fencing sword. Use of this type of pusher stick is required of all employees. Training in the use of the pusher stick and replacement of the wood is documented.

These corrective actions were totally implemented within 6 weeks of the injury. No similar injuries at this plant have occurred since the corrective action was taken.

Although complete corrective action was taken in this scenario, there is still good reason to believe that an attorney will be successful in seeking additional benefits under a serious and willful violation of OSHA regulations in regard to proper training and supervision. However, it is normally not the infrequent or one-time shock loss that bankrupts a company. Rather, it is repeated injuries that lead to exorbitant punitive damages for willful disregard of employees' well-being. The willful disregard is self-evident because of the frequency of accidents and the failure to take complete corrective action.

9

EMPLOYER CLAIMS MANAGEMENT

Claims management is an integral part of any effective loss control program. It is primarily a function of the employer's insurance carrier. Insurance carriers retain a staff of professional claims managers variously referred to as claims adjusters, claims representatives, or claims examiners. These people are responsible for controlling the cost of the claim and keeping the claim within the "profit envelope" set by the insurance carrier's executive management.

Employers often make the mistake of believing that insurance carriers have no incentive to manage claims as tightly as possible because they gain some sort of tax advantage by holding open large reserves, or they may gain a greater proportion of the premium by maintaining high reported incurred losses, thus raising experience modifiers and concomitantly the total premium. In fact, private insurance carriers have no incentive to maintain high reserves or to allow incurred expenses to become excessive. Private carriers must maintain reserve minimums by state law. An insurance carrier seldom earns an underwriting profit. That is, most insurance carriers are paying out in claims and legal expenses from 10 percent to 15 percent more money than they are taking in in premium dollars. Private insurance carriers earn profits from the interest collected on the premium dollars before those premium dollars are paid out in claims.

State regulations require that all carriers maintain what is known as a *policyholders surplus*. In general, though some states may have more or less stringent requirements, this means that the carrier must have $1 in policyholder surplus for every $2 of written premium. *Written premium* is that premium shown on the insurance policy at the beginning of the premium year. *Earned premium* is that premium actually collected. As the policy year progresses, earned premium on each policy goes up while written premium goes down.

Insurance carriers have only two choices of where to place premium dollars. They may place them in a claims reserve account, or they may place them in a policyholder surplus account. Claims reserves must be readily accessible to pay claims as needed. Therefore, interest earned on those monies are the lowest rates available, as is normal for liquid access accounts. Policyholder surplus investments may be in any approved investment with a minimum cash reserve for claims reserves should that be necessary.

These requirements create a "cash hungry" scenario for all private insurance carriers. They have a strong incentive to ensure positive cash flow and avoid having to tap into policyholder surplus investments to meet administrative costs or claims costs. Therefore, all private insurance carriers wish to set claims reserves as low as possible and close out open claims as soon as possible in order to move claims reserves dollars to policyholder surplus, or at least avoid having to re-fund claims reserves.

Some employers are under the mistaken impression that there is a tax incentive for insurance carriers to maintain reserves as long as possible because dollars held in claims reserves are tax deferred or tax deductible when actually paid out. However, this tax incentive pales in comparison to the improved cash flow and profits that can be earned when maximum investment potential is realized by good claims management and profits from long-term investment. On the other hand, state-operated insurance funds have both an administrative disadvantage in comparison with private carriers and a monetary disincentive to close claims as soon as possible and maintain reserves as low as possible. State insurance funds operate on a budget set by the state legislature's Ways and Means Committee. This budget is based on the expenses and reserves of the prior year's insurance fund extrapolated to a future year's needs. A state-operated insurance fund will often be "short handed" because hiring is constrained by budgetary considerations. Hence a typical claims examiner for a state insurance fund will handle 350 to 400 cases. This compares adversely to a private carrier, whose claims examiners usually handle 150 to 200 cases each. As a result of this difference, state claims examiners do not have the time to manage all claims as well as a private carrier's claims examiners even when competence levels are equal.

Furthermore, since the following year's budget is based on the previous year's expenses and reserves, there is a disincentive to keep reserves as low as possible, or to close them out as soon as possible. The greater the reserve and expense profile, the greater the budget. Since these budgetary dollars come from the general tax fund, we see a budget inflationary cycle typical of all bureaucratic operations. In states where dividends are paid to policyholders, there have been occasions when claims paid, expenses, reserves, and policyholder dividends exceed the dollars collected in premiums. The obvious explanation for this fiscal sleight of hand is the availability of rescue dollars from the general tax fund in the form of next year's increased budgetary allocations. Taxpayers, of course, are seldom aware of these inequities because financial reports of claims reserves and policyholder dividends are combined with administrative expenses and claims paid, and further justified by well-timed news releases of state-operated rating bureaus indicating escalating claims costs.

Regardless of whether an employer is covered by a state insurance fund or by a private carrier, the employer's individual claims cost profile can be significantly improved through the application of loss control principles and good employer claims management. The first step toward effective employer claims management is a thorough investigation of the accident. Without a thorough investigation, effective application of employer claims management techniques is virtually impossible.

FIRST REPORT SUBMISSION

In all states, an employer is required to file a first report of injury with the insurance carrier within a specified period of time, normally within 5 working days of the injury. Insurance carriers, regardless of their relative efficiency, need a certain amount of lead time to process bills and issue disability payments. When claims reports are delayed to the carrier, payments will be delayed to the injured employee. If payments are delayed to the injured employee, there is a much greater chance that the employee will seek or accept the services of an attorney. If the employee retains an attorney, claims costs will increase at least 50 percent, and claims reserves will rise as well. It therefore behooves the employer to establish a claims processing system to file claims within the appropriate time requirements.

When an employer anticipates, or learns that due to circumstances beyond its control a claim report will be delayed, the insurance carrier should be contacted with a verbal explanation of the anticipated claim and a reason for the delay. Employers should not wait to make contact and establish rapport with the insurance carrier. The employer's claims personnel should learn who the claims examiner is before the need arises to report a claim. They should also learn the name of the claims supervisor. As a group, claims supervisors have a more stable employment record than claims examiners. Claims examiners tend to move from company to company as workloads increase or to improve their salary profile. Therefore, the employer should make a courtesy contact call to the claims examiner approximately every 90 days. Claims examiners receive hundreds of calls per day, and nearly all are calls of complaint. The verbal abuse that many endure would surprise the average employer. Receiving a friendly call from time to time is like an oasis in a dessert of pain. The resulting improved claims service to the employer more than justifies the effort.

Most insurance carriers assign claims examiners by employer alphabetical assignment. However, some will assign claims based upon claimant alphabetical assignment and/or the claims examiner's relative experience. Under these circumstances, it will not always be possible for the employer to establish a rapport with the individual claims examiner prior to an actual claim being submitted. Such rapport must then be established between the claims supervisor or manager and the employer.

At insurance carriers, all mail is received by a Mail Department. There it is opened and directed to the appropriate operational department (in this example, the Claims Department). When it arrives at the Claims Department, the contents of the envelope are removed by a clerk and logged. The clerk will then forward the contents to the appropriate claims examiner. The examiner will review the claim report and make a decision as to whether or not the claim is a medical only claim, or will require disability payments. Medical only claims are usually handled by less experienced claims representatives. The claims examiner will also have to decide if the claim requires investigation.

There are a number of opportunities for the claim report to be diverted or lost. To avoid these pitfalls, the following procedure should always be followed:

- Include the words "Claims Department" and the name of the claims examiner, whenever possible, on the face of the envelope.
- The name of the claims examiner should be written at the top of the claims form in the upper margin and preferably in a different color ink than the body of the report. If the name of the claims examiner is not known, the employer should call the claims supervisor to find out to whom to direct the claim report. Always get a name.
- If the claim is serious and the employer anticipates lost time, attach a complete investigative report, or if the investigative report is not yet finished, a brief explanation of what occurred and an indication that the complete report will follow. This will alert the claims examiner that the claim is serious and not a medical only claim. The severity of the claim is often misunderstood by a tired or harried claims examiner who really would rather not add one more problem to the stack.
- If the claim is questionable, follow the above procedure and write in the margin of the claims report in red ink the words "Very Questionable Claim—Please Investigate."

FIRST REPORT SUBMISSION FOLLOW-UP

The employer should date the follow-up for 5 working days after the day the first report of injury is put into the mail. At that time the employer should contact the insurance carrier and ask to speak to the claims examiner to whom the claim report was sent. Verify that the report was received, and ask if there is any additional information the examiner would like. If the employer has additional information, this should be briefly described and then forwarded as soon as possible. Do not burden the claims examiner with a lengthy description of the additional information you are sending, and do not ask about the progress of the claim at this time. Your contact should be as brief as possible. If you waste the claims examiner's time, you will not get through easily again. Future contacts should be made only if additional information pertinent to the claim is gathered.

It is a good idea to check on the progress of the claim from time to time. This should be done no more frequently than every 90 days. If the claim has been received with accurate reporting and support material, you can be assured that management will proceed normally on most legitimate claims. With questionable claims there are no hard rules, but again 90-day contacts should be all that are required. The questionable claim is the most serious and costly because any cost for illegitimate injuries is excessive. Employers often become frustrated when employees receive benefits on claims the employer considers to be fraudulent or out of proportion to the true nature of the injury. They are frustrated because the laws are weighted on the behalf of the employee, because of the unfortunate inequities perpetrated by employers before the advent of our present compensation system.

Nevertheless, pertinent additional information learned by the employer needs to be communicated to the insurance carrier. If an employer learns that an employee on disability is working at another job, this should be communicated to the carrier. However, hearsay reports are valueless. A carrier needs to know where the employee is working and have some idea of when. Private investigators hired to photograph a moon-lighting employee are very expensive and will increase the cost of the claim. Do not call the insurance carrier unless you have specific and verifiable information. The more detailed your information, the better job your carrier can do in protecting your mutual interests.

Employers sometimes feel that their carriers should be completely responsible for the investigation of a questionable claim. And so they should. But the practicality of the matter is that an employer will often have access to information not available to a carrier, even with a full-time investigative person in the field. Employers need to realize that the law makes it very difficult for a carrier to deny benefits to an injured employee even when the claim is very questionable. Nevertheless, the employer should not become discouraged. Employees who seek to work the system attempt to do so through employers who make it easy for them to fake a claim. The stronger the employer's loss control efforts, the less an employee will be inclined to fake a claim with that employer. Insurance fraud is a felony in all states, and employees who fake claims are well aware of this fact. Often they will avoid the employer with an effective loss control program. The people who are inclined to fake claims share information and tend to gravitate toward employers with little or no loss control.

If the employer finds it is having communications problems with the carrier in regard to reaching the claims examiner, receiving answers to questions, or having telephone calls returned, personnel people should first try to resolve these difficulties through the claims supervisor. If an attempt to resolve the problem through the claims supervisor fails, the employer should contact the insurance agent. It is important to choose an agency with the facilities to handle resolution of communication difficulties. Some agencies have developed loss control personnel who will also maintain rapport with the carrier's claims departments, as well as provide loss control assistance to clients. Such an agency will prove very valuable as an adjunct to an employer's loss control efforts.

To aid in resolving communications problems, it is important to maintain a communications log. Each claims file should have a communications log which indicates the date and time telephone calls were made or received, the person spoken to, and a brief description of action to be taken. If it then becomes necessary to resolve a communications problem, all pertinent data will be available concerning past efforts.

TREATMENT FOLLOW-UP

Insurance company processing procedures are normally designed to trigger scrutiny if any one bill exceeds $300. As a result, some medical people have taken advantage of this "trigger level" by having patients return again and again for treatment billed below the $300 amount. It is not unusual for an employee to be given a doctor's release to return to work while continuing to receive treatment. Employers are unaware of the ongoing treatment until they receive a year-end accounting from the insurance carrier. Employers need to establish a treatment follow-up procedure on all injured employees to avoid this scenario. The procedure is as follows:

• The employer should always contact the treating physician following initial diagnosis and treatment. The purpose of this contact is to find out what kind of injury or illness the employee has sustained, the treatment anticipated, and estimated length of time to end of treatment. If the estimate does not sound reasonable, the insurance carrier's claims examiner should be contacted for advice and possibly to arrange for a second opinion.

• At least once every 30 days while the employee is being treated, the treating facility should be contacted for a progress report. Again, if at any time the progress report does not seem reasonable, the claims examiner should be asked for advice.

• After the employee has returned to work, the medical facility should be contacted to find out if treatment is complete, or if follow-up visits are required.

Ideally, when an employer has a designated physician program in place, with good physician rapport, progress reports will be sent automatically by the treating facility. It is important for an employer to receive a doctor's release before allowing an employee to return to work. If the employee returns to work without a release and is subsequently injured further because he or she returned to work too soon, the employer may be held responsible. This kind of aggravated injury has resulted in legitimate workers' compensation claims developing from non-work-related injuries. Penalties have been assessed against employers in the form of fines and/or punitive damages for "requiring" an employee to come back to work before the doctor had released him or her.

PREEXISTING CONDITIONS

Occasionally, employees will seek treatment on their own for conditions which they believe to be unrelated to the work they are doing for their present employer. While they are on sick leave, it may come to the attention of their current employer that the preexisting condition may be aggravated by the work the employee is now doing, thus triggering a workers' compensation claim. The employee then wishes to return to work after treatment for the present non-work-related condition. The employer does not know whether to bring the employee back to work or terminate him or her to avoid the chance of a future claim.

Generally speaking, it is not possible to terminate an employee under these conditions without running the very good risk of sustaining a wrongful termination lawsuit. However, OSHA regulations specifically constrain the employer from placing any employee in a position where he or she will knowingly be injured. To resolve the conflict, the following policy and procedure must be in place:

- Make certain that all candidates fill out complete employment applications.
- Make certain that the application contains the disclosure that any false or misleading statement is grounds for termination.
- Make certain that the application or written employer policy is signed and accepted by the employee and contains the disclosure that any preexisting medical condition which is discovered subsequent to hire and which might be aggravated by the work the employee is doing for the employer will require a medical examination, at the employer's expense, to ensure that the employee will not be further injured as the result of the duties. The employee will be placed on an unpaid leave of absence until such medical examination is conducted and the resulting diagnosis indicates that the employee may work safely with the preexisting condition.
- If a preexisting medical condition is subsequently discovered, the employee should be examined as soon as possible

by a physician recommended by the employer's insurance carrier.

- If an employee cannot pass the medical exam, he or she must be moved into a position that poses no risk of aggravation of the preexisting condition, or terminated. A preexisting condition, aggravated by work currently being done by an employee, is a legitimate workers' compensation claim.
- Before terminating any employee under these circumstances, contact an attorney familiar with wrongful termination cases. Case law is constantly changing and varies significantly from state to state. Follow your attorney's advice.

CLAIMS MONITORING

Incurred expense by an insurance carrier on a given claim is the expense which is reported to the state rating bureau and ultimately affects the experience modification of premium paid by the employer for workers' compensation insurance. *Incurred expense* is defined as the amount of money paid and reserved by an insurance carrier for any given claim. The incurred expense is reported to the state rating bureau between 90 and 180 days after the close of the policy year. However, typically insurance company loss runs reflect only the status of the claim at the close of the policy year. This status may or may not accurately reflect the statistical report of incurred expenses that will be sent to the state rating bureau.

It is important for the employer to do the following to ensure that a fair estimate of incurred expense for all the employer's claims is reported:

- If the employer buys insurance from an independent agent, the employer should choose an agent with a workers' compensation claims monitoring service. Typically such an agent will have customer service representatives who monitor loss runs produced by the insurance carrier and follow through on the claims' status for reporting purposes. If the employer buys insurance direct from a company, it is imperative that the employer maintain good rapport with the carrier's claims management personnel.
- Choose a carrier that produces a readable loss run at least quarterly and will provide it to the employer. Such a loss run

should include a final run for the policy year delivered to the employer no later than 45 days following the close of the policy year.

- The employer should review the loss run and note the open claims which in the opinion of the employer should be closed because the employee is back to work and where follow-up has indicated that all treatment has ceased.

- The employer, through the independent agent or directly through the carrier's claims management personnel, should request that all such open claims be closed and receive a commitment that they will be closed prior to being reported to the state rating bureau.

The latter may be a negotiable point in some cases. Claims examiners must make a decision whether or not a claim will reopen in the future. These decisions are based primarily upon statistical information on similar claims and the examiner's own personal experience. If the claims examiner feels the claim must remain open because of anticipated future expenses, the next step is negotiation of the reserve.

Nothing will be gained for the employer by arguing with claims management personnel over the validity of recurrence. Neither the claims examiner nor the employer can accurately predict the future, but certainly the probability of expense is negotiable. It is here that an experienced independent agent with a good claims monitoring service is particularly valuable. Not only can the agent negotiate more objectively, because it is not their experience modifier at stake, but he or she may also invoke the weight of agency business, which will have a positive effect on the claims examiner's decision.

Ultimately it is the total dollars an insurance carrier has in its reserve which dictates its ability to handle future reopened claims without tapping into its policyholder surplus. And those total dollars are produced by premiums from future business. An independent agent supplies far more future dollars to a carrier than any single insured employer. Finally, it should be obvious that claims reserve negotiations and assurances of closed claims are really a variation of "closing the barn door after the horse has left." Effective loss control to prevent claims in the first place is a far more effective method of reducing experience modifiers and premiums.

10

LOSS CONTROL
INCENTIVE AWARD
PROGRAMS

Incentive programs are a valuable adjunct to any employer's loss control efforts. An incentive program may involve recognition awards, monetary awards, merchandise awards, or any combination thereof. The most important facet of the incentive program is the degree of recognition and prestige employees receive as a result of qualifying for the incentive award.

The primary purpose of any incentive program is to generate an esprit de corps among the employees and a safety-conscious attitude. The esprit de corps is created by the fact that as the program progresses, more and more employees are recognized for their safety and performance efforts. At first, a small special group is created which all employees outside the group wish to join. As the group grows larger, the corresponding esprit de corps also grows. Eventually all employees have joined the group, and the esprit de corps is now transferred to the company as a whole—that is, pride in being a part of the company, rather than just a group of people within the company.

By carefully designing the incentive program, it is possible to establish an ongoing situation where employees develop company pride and small group pride as different levels of the incentive program are reached. The incentive program must never reach a level beyond which an employee becomes stagnant. There must always be another goal to be reached.

A safety-conscious attitude is promoted if the incentive program is tied into safety efforts, results, and responsibilities. Employees seeking to reach various levels within the incentive program must also become more and more involved in safety and accident prevention in order to reach the desired goals. This constant involvement will, over time, instill a safety-conscious attitude in the employees, and a safety-conscious attitude is the single most important factor in reducing and eliminating work-related accidents and injuries. Regardless of what mechanical or physical cause may be attributed to an accident or injury, there is always a human element. Absolutely no accident occurs without some human contribution. Most frequently, the employee involved in the accident has contributed to the accident.

Prevention of accidents and injuries can best be accomplished by ensuring that employees think about safety ramifications before attempting to complete a task or operate a piece of equipment. This simple idea is so often accepted as pure common sense employers forget that "common sense" is really only a synonym for "experience," and experience comes only from training and exposure to a variety of circumstances over time.

A safety-conscious attitude involves more than just the ability to recognize a hazard or a dangerous situation. It involves the ability to decide on the safest procedure for completing a task, and to recognize one's own limitations. Employers must be careful to promote an attitude that safety is primary among both line and supervisory personnel. No employee should ever be too embarrassed to ask for training, or for help in performing a task in the safest manner. Development of a safety-conscious attitude in every single employee 24 hours a day is the ultimate goal of any incentive program, and of the loss control program.

Employee recognition is the single most important factor in establishing pride and employee loyalty. Recognition of a job well done is more important than monetary or material awards. This is not to say that material awards are not important, but material awards without recognition are far less effective. As with all employer policies and programs, the incentive program must be documented and all employees must be given the opportunity to participate.

DESIGNING THE LOSS CONTROL INCENTIVE PROGRAM

The first step in designing a loss control incentive program is to place a business in one of the following major categories: manufacturing, field operations, or manufacturing and field operations. While many subcategories may be assigned, all business activity will fall into one of these categories. The type of loss control incentive program chosen will depend upon the category in which the business falls.

MANUFACTURING OPERATIONS

The type of incentive program chosen for the manufacturing operation will depend upon the subcategory into which the business fits. Manufacturing operations need to be broken down into one of two subcategories: line manufacturing and custom manufacturing.

Line manufacturing of basically similar products uses repetitive machining and labor tasks. Custom manufacturing, with a variety of tasks and/or machinery, may also include R&D with a variety of lead times and production runs.

Line Manufacturing

Due to the repetitive nature of line manufacturing, boredom with the task being performed hour after hour and day after day is one of the greatest contributing factors to high employee turnover and injury. Injury is caused primarily by boredom, which leads to lack of concentration and hence an accident. Any employer with an operation that requires employees to perform the same task over and over again needs to do one or more of the following:

- Establish a policy of work station rotation to provide a variety of tasks for employees to perform.
- Where machinery is involved, make certain that the possi-

bility of injury is virtually eliminated by total safety engi-
neering of the equipment, adequate training, and good
supervision to ensure that proper operating procedures are
followed and that shortcuts are not allowed.

- Increase the frequency of breaks, including allowances for 5-
minute "stretch breaks." Stretch breaks are exactly that;
employees perform specific stretching exercises at their work
station. These are not breaks for coffee, conversation, or
other diversion. The safety director should be familiar with
an appropriate stretching routine which is taught to each
employee by his or her supervisor, who has learned the
routine from the safety director.

The line manufacturer who installs a loss control incentive
program without first accomplishing one or more of these steps
will suffer a 50 percent reduction in the effectiveness of the
incentive program.

Employee turnover is a major consideration for line manufacturers. High employee turnover will result in a higher
frequency of accidents, because new employees have a much
higher risk of injury due to inexperience. Boredom is less of a
contributing factor to the injury of the newer employee.
Reduction of boredom will not offset the increase of risk from
inexperience. High employee turnover also significantly increases the employer's costs and reduces efficiency, due to the
need constantly to hire and train new people. Line manufacturers with high employee turnover are constantly a little
short-handed, which overloads other employees and creates
another risk factor when overloaded employees attempt to rush
through a task in order to be "caught up." Therefore, it is in the
area of reduction of employee turnover that the loss control
incentive program is most effective for the employer. This in
turn has an indirect relationship to the loss control of line
operations.

It is important that all employees feel they are a part of the
loss control incentive group, even though they may not yet
have reached the first goal level of the program. This is
accomplished by the overall loss control program of the
employer, including training efforts, the written safety policy,
and the signed employee compliance statement.

To reinforce this feeling of group commitment, the employer needs to display a sign indicating the number of days that have elapsed since the last "lost time" injury. It is important to emphasize "lost time" injuries in association with the elapsed time sign and the first level of the loss control incentive program. As the employee progresses through the various incentive levels, the importance of degree of injury becomes more finely tuned, to the extent that near injuries are calculated in the equation. Associated with the "days since last lost time accident" sign should be an incentive in which all employees may participate and which occurs regularly at 60- to 90-day intervals. These full staff participation incentives should not always occur at exactly the same time. Varying the frequency of the incentive between 60 and 90 days is beneficial. However, at each incentive award it must be made clear that the award is associated with the good safety record attained by *all* employees.

These group incentive awards may consist of:

- Serving ice cream, cake or other food treats.
- A half-hour longer lunch break on one particular day.
- Shutting down a half-hour early on one particular day.
- Having live entertainment at the lunch hour.

Varying the incentive chosen is also beneficial, so that employees will look forward to the next incentive with enthusiasm and curiosity.

It is always important for the employee to know from the onset what to expect. Therefore, it should be stated in the written incentive policy that group incentives will occur at varying intervals. On the day following the incentive award a notice should be posted indicating the interval to the next award, but not what the next award will be. As a rule of thumb, the more expensive or impressive the award, the greater the period of time until the next award. The employer should not fall into the trap of trying to "outdo" the previous award. If the operation has gone 90 days and received live entertainment at lunch as the award, the next incentive should occur at 70 days and be a little less expensive or impressive. In this way employees will not become conditioned to expect greater and greater awards and will not become jaded by the program.

Individual Reward Levels

The first incentive level should be attainable within 6 months of hire for new employees and 6 months of initial program inception for current employees. The first level is a recognition award consisting of complimenting the employee before the peer group and presenting the person with a tangible token of recognition, such as:

- A "safety" pin with the company logo which can be worn on any article of clothing.
- A "safety" patch with the company logo to be attached to uniform overalls, shirt, or jacket.
- A jacket or T-shirt with the company logo in the first-level color to which higher-level recognition awards may be attached.

In designing the incentive program it is important that thought is given to all levels of recognition. Many employers will present a company jacket to employees at the first level to which patches or pins may be attached as other levels are attained. The employees with the most patches and pins have greater prestige, and their level of attainment is desired by lower-level employees. Some employers will use colors to designate levels associated with jackets, or T-shirts which carry company logos and safety slogans. The rewards are limited only by the employer's imagination and budget.

The subsequent award levels should occur at 6-month intervals indefinitely. All award levels should include employee recognition in front of peers. However, as the employees progress upward through the award levels, their involvement in the company loss control program and their level of personal accident-free operation becomes more a part of the award criteria. The monetary value of subsequent award levels is of less significance than the criteria for attainment of each successive level. However, at least once a year, beginning at the end of the second year, a material prize or monetary award should accompany the recognition award. Again, the size or type of material award is limited only by the employer's imagination and budget.

The second level occurs at one year and involves recognition/ token with increased involvement in the employer's loss control program. This increased involvement should include participation in the ongoing safety inspection program. Participation should be limited to no more than eight weekly inspections and no less than three weekly inspections. The safety inspections should be conducted consecutively, as it will often take an employee two to three inspections to learn the process and to begin making appropriate suggestions for improvement.

During the second year, each employee should be able to submit one valid loss control suggestion, as well as avoid any lost time injury to reach second-year individual award levels. By the third year, an employee may qualify for third-year award levels through involvement in safety inspections with loss control suggestions, or accident investigation with suggestions, or attendance at safety committee meetings, or writing two or more safety slogans for posting, or contributing one or more loss control suggestions not associated with safety inspections, or other contributions to the improvement of the employer's loss control efforts. By the fourth year, and in every year thereafter, criteria for attaining award levels should include contribution to the overall program as indicated above, and also training of less experienced employees in the safe accomplishment of tasks.

Naturally, regardless of any additional contributions an employee may make, not being involved in an accident is a prerequisite for reaching any given award level. Although monetary awards are of less value in raising the level of safety consciousness than recognition awards, their value in reducing absenteeism is unique to the line manufacturing operation. Incentives involving monetary increases on an hourly basis should require no more than one month of no lost time to qualify for the award. Extending the award beyond that period will be counterproductive. Conversely, paying the award more frequently than bimonthly reduces its effectiveness.

Interestingly, the monetary award has little to do with reinforcing a safety-conscious attitude. After a month or two employees come to expect the award as a part of their normal remuneration. However, this type of award is very effective in reducing employee absenteeism for a period of 120 to 180 days. Beyond the 180-day point its effectiveness is reduced, and some employee absenteeism may be expected. However, when the incentive award is missed at the next applicable paycheck, a reinforcement of the need to be on the job may occur and remain in effect for another extended period of time.

Custom Manufacturing

While the basic principles of loss control incentive award programs apply to any operation, the custom manufacturing operation will require some distinct variation to the program designed for the line manufacturing operation.

In custom manufacturing boredom is not a contributing factor to injury or high employee turnover. Injury frequency is often a result of the fact that the operation is so varied that each new item requires a learning period. Even long-term employees may run a higher risk of injury due to the lack of experience in manufacturing the new item. Monetary awards to reduce absenteeism are generally of little value because pride of workmanship in the new product is a much greater incentive. Therefore, the emphasis on quality and craftsmanship should be tied into the attainment of successive award levels, and definitely be a part of the peer recognition award system.

The safety inspection program will require close monitoring by the safety director, with greater emphasis on safe operating procedures and training. Completion of training checklists associated with each new item of manufacture or each new procedure is very important. Under no circumstances should qualification for any award level be tied to the speed with which an employee learns a new task. If such a correlation is made in the minds of employees, they will cease to seek additional training when they are not sure of a procedure. Tying in supervisory award levels to completed training documentation is a good idea to ensure supervisors do not assume an employee knows how to manufacture a new item simply because there is great similarity between the new item and a previously manufactured item.

Housekeeping is an important safety inspection item, and

should be emphasized especially where research and development operations are in progress. Employees developing new products will have a tendency to "rig" operations in the process of testing or developing a new product. This can result in a variety of injury exposures to the developers themselves and to employees not directly involved in the project. In research and development firms incentive systems are often associated with the development of a viable product or procedure for manufacturing a product economically. This recognition and/or reward often overshadows the relevant safety considerations associated with the new product. Therefore, it is important to make certain that the development and use of safe operating procedures is projected as equally important to the final product. No employee should receive recognition or an award for developing a product or procedure that has serious safety flaws in the manufacturing process.

Supervisor Incentives

When designing any type of loss control incentive award program, you need to keep in mind the fact that supervisors play a unique role in the effectiveness of the employer's loss control program and the effectiveness of the loss control incentive award program. Supervisors are the first level of safe operating procedures enforcement. Without the close supervision of the employees for whom they are responsible, neither the loss control program nor the loss control incentive award program can be effective.

Supervisors who successfully supervise employees who do not have accidents need to be rewarded monetarily as well as through peer recognition. When their employees have accidents, they should share in the employer's loss through a reduction of the monetary incentive that would otherwise accrue to them. Monetary awards given to supervisors should be given discreetly, because line employees will only become jealous of the supervisor's increased remuneration. While it may become generally known through the grapevine that supervisors receive a monetary incentive for accident-free operation in their departments, this should not be made a part of the peer recognition program. However, an injury occurring to a supervisor's employee should not disqualify the supervisor from attaining a personal recognition/token award level, for two reasons:

1. A supervisor can exert only so much control over any employee. To a great extent, the safety and well-being of the employee falls upon the employee's shoulders, especially in regard to following the supervisor's instructions. The supervisor should not be penalized because of the failings of a supervised employee so far as their personal safety awareness is concerned, whereas the monetary reward reflects the overall success of their supervisory ability in regard to safety.

2. Some employees would take a perverse delight in preventing a supervisor from attaining a personal recognition level by purposely having an accident to get even for a personality conflict they may be having with the supervisor. Therefore, if for no other reason, no employee should be given the opportunity to use the loss control incentive award program as a tool of retribution.

FIELD OPERATIONS

The basic ideas for line manufacturing operations will also apply to field operations. However, here again there are some intrinsic differences that need to be delineated. Field operations may be broken down into two subcategories: construction and related activities, and service operations that would include outside sales. The basic difference between the two subcategories has to do with individual supervision of field employees and location of a fixed construction site. Outside sales and service employees are generally not individually supervised in the field and generally do not have a fixed location. Construction and related duty employees generally are individually supervised and do have a fixed site. If a construction employee is not individually supervised and/or does not have a fixed site in the field, the loss control incentive award program for that employee would more closely resemble the program designed for the outside sales force.

Service and Outside Sales Force Operations

The greatest risk exposure to an outside sales force involves vehicular accidents. Any loss control incentive award program should place strong emphasis on vehicular safety. This emphasis should include regular fleet inspections of company and private vehicles for maintenance and housekeeping. Even though employees supply their own vehicles, the appearance and maintenance of that vehicle will project the image of the employer. More important, any accident involving the employee during working hours or while on company business will involve the employer in related liability, if only because ultimately the employer is the "deep pocket" for financial compensation.

A checklist should be developed for fleet inspections with minimum standards that are taken into consideration for reaching any given award level. Regular checks of the employee's Department of Motor Vehicle records should be required. However, to avoid charges of invasion of privacy, employees should be required to sign a statement of compliance in regard to Department of Motor Vehicle record checks, and be required to bring a copy of such checks themselves on an annual basis. DMV records are now considered important by insurance carriers underwriting employer's general liability insurance not only when company vehicles are involved, but also when employees' vehicles are used for company business. Employees with more than three moving violations or with any Driving Under the Influence violations will have an adverse effect on the cost of general liability insurance and may disqualify an employer from receiving a competitive quote on workers' compensation insurance. Employees working in the field need to realize that their off-time driving habits are as important as their work-time driving habits and that those associated records will affect their qualification for a given level of loss control incentive awards. How to relate the driver information and fleet inspection information to the incentive program is up to the employer. However, in all cases the qualification policy should be set down in writing and be consistently applied to all employees equally to avoid charges of discrimination.

Another important factor in outside sales operations is the customer environment in which a sales representative is making a presentation. In many cases sales representatives will meet customer personnel at work sites or production sites whose very nature presents a risk of injury to the uninformed. Injuries may occur to sales personnel while making a sales call as the result of the customer's operations. It is important that the employer instill a safety-conscious attitude in the sales force because it is impossible for the employer to anticipate every hazardous situation the sales representative may encounter. Including safety topics in sales force meetings, having the sales force involved in loss control incentive award programs, and emphasizing fleet safety, product demonstration safety, and involvement in the employer's overall loss control efforts will be beneficial to raising the safety-consciousness of the sales force.

Construction Site Operations

Construction operations offer one of the greatest opportunities for implementation of loss control procedures and loss control incentive award programs. The construction site is a constantly changing environment with overlapping operations often run by a variety of subcontractors. These operations present a risk of injury generally greater than any fixed manufacturing operation, and they also present the opportunity for a varied and interesting loss control opportunity.

The general contractor must keep in mind that by OSHA and labor law regulations, it is the general contractor who is responsible for the safety and well-being of all individuals at the job site, regardless of their status as a subcontractor or their individual insurance coverage.

All the basics of loss control apply at the construction site:

- Safety inspections are essential to monitor safe operating procedures for both workers and visitors to the site.
- Near accident and accident investigations must be conducted as thoroughly as possible to protect the interests of the general contractor.
- Progress logs and photographs should be maintained.
- By regulation, safety meetings must be held at least every 10 days at the site.
- Centralized hiring is essential.
- Designated medical facilities are required by regulation, as is a means of communicating with those facilities in the event of an emergency.

The application of a loss control incentive award program can be very beneficial to both the job site safety record and time to completion. The most successful job site loss control incentive award programs involve award levels that occur approximately every 3 weeks and are purely recognition/token award programs with a material award in some cases being provided at the completion of the job. Material awards are normally offered if the job lasts 6 months or longer and occur at 6-month intervals. Some employers will provide a material award on a 9-month job site at 6 months and then again at the end of the job. Material awards are provided only to workers who are on the job from inception to completion and those subcontractors who are on the job for 6 months or longer.

Some employers will factor in awards based on the timely completion of the job within budget, but this approach must be coupled with a solid safety inspection program to avoid the tendency of workers to rush when they get a little behind, which increases the risk of injury. As with the manufacturing award programs, peer recognition is of primary importance to the success of the program. Tokens of recognition are almost limitless, and may include:

• T-shirts of varying colors for levels on attainment
• Hats
• Decals for hard hats
• Pins for shirts and hats
• Jackets
• Work boots

As with the manufacturing programs, individual worker involvement in the safety inspections, safety meetings, and corrective actions should be an essential element in qualifying for higher award levels.

The use of a loss control incentive award program can significantly increase the total effectiveness of the employer's overall loss control efforts, reduce the amount of employee turnover, increase the group pride of all employees, and improve the efficiency and hence the profitability of the entire operation.

11

OTHER LOSS CONTROL IDEAS

This chapter presents a variety of loss control and safety ideas for the purpose of stimulating "loss control thinking." The ideas follow no particular order and may have no specific applicability to a given reader's individual needs. However, the fact that thought is given to the concepts involved in each of the following ideas will result in readers' developing ideas specific to their individual needs.

INDIVIDUAL SAFETY EQUIPMENT

Weightlifter Belts

Four-inch-wide weightlifter belts have been found to be very useful in reducing work-related back injuries caused by repeated bending and/or lifting. These belts come in a variety of materials, including leather, nylon, Lycra, canvas, and any combination thereof. Contrary to popular belief, the belts do not support the back. They do, however, reduce the strain placed on the connective tissues attached to the bones of the lower back. Where relatively heavy weight is involved, the belts also help to support the lower abdominal muscles and equalize internal pressures.

The primary cause of common low back pain is inflammation of the connective tissues that join the flat low back muscles to the bones of the lower spine. Movements such as bending, twisting, stretching, and lifting put significant strain on these lower back connective tissues even when proper lifting techniques are used. Over time, the tissues become inflamed and cause lower back pain. This is compensated for by injured workers with attempts to hold themselves in positions that reduce the pain. The result is further inflammation through poor body mechanics and/or more serious injury. Use of weightlifter belts greatly reduces the strain and fatigue that results in lost time.

Weightlifter belts are presently being successfully worn by warehouse workers, construction workers, truckers, heavy equipment drivers, manufacturing workers, mechanics, hotel housekeeping personnel, and anyone whose work requires repeated bending and/or lifting or who presently experiences low back pain due to connective tissue strain.

Weightlifter belts cannot prevent or cure damage done to vertebral discs due to compression injury or cumulative trauma. However, some workers with deteriorating disc conditions have reported pain relief while wearing the belts.

Safety Glasses and Goggles

It is common practice for workers to wear safety glasses and/or goggles whenever they are using tools that generate flying foreign objects which can lodge in or injure their eyes. However, this safety equipment can be valuable in other instances as well.

One of the most common causes of lost time is blowing dust and debris getting into a worker's eye and requiring a vist to the first aid clinic to have the foreign object removed. Often the treatment will require a patch on the eye and one or two days' recovery. This treatment results in lost time expense to both employer and employee. The employer may have to pay overtime to someone else to stay on schedule, and the employee is not off long enough to recoup lost time earnings, as he or she does not qualify for benefits for at least three days.

Wearing wraparound safety glasses anytime windy conditions are encountered is a good idea and a simple way to reduce lost time due to injury. Workers who work outdoors or who often go outside from an indoor environment should be issued safety glasses and encouraged to wear them whenever the wind is blowing.

The newer safety glass styles are very attractive and can be ordered as tinted sunglasses as well. Workers presently benefitting from this approach include construction workers, truckers, heavy equipment drivers, mechanics, gas station attendants, road crews, and anyone exposed to blowing dust conditions.

Hearing Protection

It is now common practice for manufacturing operations to conduct noise level tests whenever there is any question in regard to employee exposure to excessive sound. OSHA regulations are based upon time-weighted averages and are adequate, when adhered to, to guard against permanent hearing loss. However, few employers realize the significant increase in fatigue created by noisy environments which are below ear protection threshold requirements. Whenever an employee is exposed to relatively continuous sound levels in excess of 75db, fatigue is increased. Fatigue in and of itself is a major cause of work-related injuries. When workers becomes fatigued, they are less likely to maintain a safety-conscious attitude and therefore are more likely to be injured.

All employees exposed to sound levels in excess of 75db should be provided with hearing protection and encouraged to wear the protection while they are working. A variety of protection devices should be made available, as different ear sizes accommodate different protection devices. And many employees prefer to switch between two different devices, such as earplugs and earmuffs, because any form of ear protection begins to annoy the wearer after a prolonged period of time. Such an annoyance is equally as serious a contributing factor to some injuries as is fatigue.

Employees should be discouraged from using personal stereo tape players to "drown out" work environment noise exposure. If such an approach is used, it will definitely cause the worker to be exposed to sound, in this case music, in excess of 75db and in many cases causes exposure to sound levels far above the OSHA time-weighted threshold levels, even when such threshold levels were not being exceeded by the work environment noise level.

Personal Protective Equipment: Employee Responsibilities

Employees should be issued all appropriate personal protective equipment, and trained in the use and maintenance of such equipment. Each piece of equipment should be assigned a reasonable specific lifetime, and employees should be made aware that they are responsible for the equipment during its specific life. If the equipment is lost, damaged due to negligence, or misplaced, the employee is responsible for purchasing a replacement. Naturally, if the equipment is damaged or destroyed while protecting the person from an injury, it would be the employer's responsibility to replace the equipment.

When employees are given responsibility for their own equipment, it becomes more important to them and as a result they are more likely to use the equipment.

WEATHER

Cold Weather

Cold weather conditions present many opportunities for a worker to be injured, both on and off the job. At the onset of winter every employer should conduct a safety meeting with all employees to discuss the increased risks of both on and off the job injuries due to cold weather conditions. Cold weather safety meetings should include discussion of:

- Dark mornings
- Vehicle lighting
- Engine warmups
- Allowing time for the brain to wake up in the morning
- Winter driving conditions, including ice, snow, rain, fog
- Body heat: how to maintain it, warmups before work, proper clothing

Many employers include cold weather discussion as part of all safety meetings conducted during cold weather months.

Darkness. Normally cold weather is assoicated with winter conditions and the fact that it is dark early in the morning when workers are driving to work. Often it is still dark at the workplace or job site when they arrive. It is important to remind workers to use extra caution to avoid falling over objects when they first arrive.

Vehicles. Both company and personal vehicles will need extra startup attention during cold weather. All windows should be thoroughly defrosted and de-iced prior to driving to work in the morning. Many accidents are caused because the driver did not see another vehicle due to obstructed vision.

Window blankets consisting of insulation sandwiched and sealed between two sheets of plastic will, under most circumstances, eliminate the need to scrape ice from front and rear windows. These blankets can easily be made or may be bought commercially through most vehicle parts after market catalogs. The blankets are placed across the front and rear windows with their end flaps held in place by shutting them in the vehicle doors. Just before leaving in the morning the blankets are removed and stowed in the trunk or other storage compartment.

All vehicle lights should be operating, and extra lights added if fog is frequently encountered. Fog lights do not improve visibility at all. They do improve the recognition factor to other drivers and reduce the chance of collision caused by another driver pulling out in front of the employee's vehicle.

All winter equipment on the vehicle—windshield wipers, defrosters, and heaters—should be in good working condition. It is especially important during the winter for employees and employers to conduct regular and frequent vehicle inspections and to make certain that the vehicles are in safe operating condition.

Driving. Employees need to be reminded to allow extra time to get to work during cold weather. Employees need to be educated to the fact that it will take a little longer to fully awaken the brain in cold weather both because of the reduced blood circulation and because brain hormones are less active during cold, dark conditions. These two factors significantly reduce alertness and reaction time in most people.

Employees should be educated to the need to arise at least an hour before leaving home and to take that time to wake up and warm up with a hot shower followed by warmup and stretching exercises. These two processes will significantly improve alertness.

Additional time to get to work must be allowed. Employees who are behind schedule will tend to focus on arriving at work on time. This not only generates excessive speed, but causes a driver to focus mostly forward, reducing side scanning and leading to accidents.

Obviously it is necessary to drive more slowly in icy or wet conditions. Being late can force an otherwise careful driver to take unsafe chances by increasing vehicle speed to make up for lost time.

Clothing. It is important to educate workers about appropriate clothing for cold weather conditions. This is especially important for younger or less experienced workers. Young people normally have higher metabolisms and more efficient blood circulation than older workers. They tend to feel the cold less and may therefore dress inappropriately for the weather conditions and later sustain a muscle injury as a result.

Workers should be apprised of the following points:

- 60 percent of heat loss is experienced through the top of the head and around the neck. Wearing a hat and turtleneck collar or simply turning the collar up on shirts and jackets will greatly reduce this heat loss.
- Layers of clothing are superior to one heavy coat. Layering clothing allows the wearer to remove a layer at a time as he or she warms up, or put the layers back on when he or she begins to cool down later.
- Warmth is maintained by the insulation of air warmed by the body. It is very important to wear a T-shirt when working in cold weather. The thin layer of air between skin and T-shirt will warm up first. The T-shirt also helps to absorb perspiration by wicking it away from the body.

- The extremities need to be protected by gloves and appropriate shoes and socks. Again, insulation is the key factor.

Warmups.   Warming up before attempting to do any physical labor in the cold is absolutely essential. Failure to warm up properly is the single greatest cause of muscle strain and sprain injuries.

Educate and encourage workers to warm up thoroughly before attempting any physical work. This begins upon arising in the morning, includes proper attire, getting to work in a warm vehicle, and doing warmup exercises before beginning work.

Caution.   Extra caution must be exercised at all job sites and work places during cold weather. Surfaces are slippery, lighting is poorer, and the cold contributes to the desire to look straight ahead to avoid turning the head and letting cold air down under the collar. The result is an increase in slip and fall injuries.

Hot Weather

During hot weather months, hot weather topics should be discussed, including:

- Drinking sufficient liquid
- Recognizing signs of heat fatigue, and/or prostration
- First aid to be administered in the event of fainting caused by heat
- Sun exposure: increased risk of skin cancer, use of sun blocks
- Appropriate clothing

PRE-WORK WARMUP EXERCISES

Muscle fibers are very much like plastic. When they are warm, they are very stretchable. When they are cold, they are brittle and tear easily. Many strain injuries are the result of repeated micro traumas to brittle muscle fiber as the result of insufficient warmup. Like a fraying rope, over time the muscle becomes weak until eventually it is torn, resulting in injury. Then scar tissue is formed which is even less flexible, and over time the injury is repeated until the pain becomes chronic.

It is common for Japanese workers to participate in warmup exercises as a group at the start of each day. Studies have shown that Japanese workers involved in such programs have approximately 60 percent fewer work-related strain injuries than non-exercising employees.

In Smyrna, Tennessee, a joint Japanese-American car manufacturing plant was built. Employees were both Japanese and American. The Japanese employees participated in group warmup exercises, while their American counterparts in general did not participate. Subsequent analysis showed that the American workers suffered approximately 49 percent more strain-related work injuries than their Japanese counterparts.

With time and the formation of friendships, many American workers began to join the morning exercise groups. Subsequent analysis showed a substantial reduction in strain-related work injuries for all exercising personnel.

LOADING DOCKS

It has been estimated that loading dock injuries account for as much as 25 percent of all industrial injuries. In the past, loading dock size was fairly standard because of trailer size regulations. However, since deregulation in 1983, trailers have increased in width from 96 to 102 inches, and from 45 feet in length to 48 feet. Additionally, internal trailer heights have been increased by lowering trailer floors to a minimum of 36 inches above the ground. As a result of these changes, accessing trailers and maneuvering loads from wide trailers through standard dock doors presents a challenging and potentially hazardous situation for forklift drivers and helpers.

Loading dock trailer access ways should be sloped toward the dock, or the dock should have a restraining device as an integral part of the dock. This is normally a hook which attaches to the ICC bar of the trailer. The vertical travel of the hook needs to be from 12 to 30 inches to accommodate the level adjustment of all present trailers. As a trailer is unloaded, the level of the trailer will adjust upward. Forklift accidents as the result of trailer creep due to the lack of a sloped access way or a restraining device account for 75 percent of all deaths from forklift accidents.

Dock levelers should also be an integral part of the loading dock, not loose. Loose levelers are a material handling hazard and can lead to accidents due to leveler creep. Dock levelers need to be wide enough to prevent forklift tires from wedging between the edge of the leveler and the trailer wall when maneuvering inside wide trailers. Wheel wedging can lead to tipover injuries and/or damage to goods being offloaded. At present, the industry is moving toward dock levelers of 6 feet 6 inches in width.

Dock levelers need to be long enough to allow for a gentle slope into the trailer. The length calculation needs to take into consideration the height of the trailer floor when unloaded. A steep dock leveler will require excessive forklift acceleration to clear the crown of the leveler. This will result in damaged trailers, goods, and people if an accident occurs due to misjudgment of required acceleration. The industry is moving toward levelers of at least 10 feet in length.

Loading dock doors should never be left fully open when not in use. Many warehouse employees leave dock doors open to allow greater air circulation, especially during warm weather. However, the doors should be lowered far enough to ensure that a forklift or person operating a pallet jack cannot inadvertently back out of the dock door while concentrating on maneuvering a load inside the warehouse. A yellow or red safety line should be painted around all dock areas. Employees should not be allowed to maneuver equipment within the painted lines unless they are loading or unloading a trailer.

Loading docks without doors should always have chain or bar barriers capable of preventing a forklift or person operating a pallet jack from going off the dock while maneuvering loads. The barriers should be in place at all times, except when goods are being loaded or unloaded from a trailer at the dock.

All openings that lead to a change in level within or outside a building should be marked with brightly colored paint. This is of particular importance when two surfaces of different levels but of the same color and/or texture meet.

Depth perception is primarily the result of contrast. Where similar colors meet, perception of elevation change is greatly reduced. Even small changes of 2 to 4 inches can lead to a severe back injury if a person steps off one level and jars down onto the next level. Trip and fall injuries can occur to someone going from a lower to a higher level.

EYEWASH STATIONS

Many secondary injuries from eye infections are caused by employees rinsing out an injured eye with an unsterile eye wash.

Water from public utility systems contains bacteria that will cause significant infections if used to rinse an injured eye. Stored water, even if bought as distilled or demineralized, can also contain unhealthy bacteria. This problem is nationwide in scope. Eyewash stations should contain only commercially available sterile saline solutions which are preserved and pH-buffered.

DOCUMENTS

Weekly Noninjury Statement

Some employers, in particular those with routine work schedules and locations, have found the use of a weekly noninjury statement valuable. The statement is signed by an employee at the end of each work week and indicates that, to the employee's knowledge, he or she has sustained no work-related injury during the prior week. This documentation gives the employee the opportunity to describe any work-related injury sustained in the prior week, or to make loss control and safety suggestions.

The purpose of this document is to remind the employee that all injuries sustained must be reported immediately. It also has the additional benefit of somewhat deterring individuals who are contemplating submitting a questionable claim. Questionable claims, as indicated earlier, normally are reported late. An employee uses such a tactic in the hope that witnesses who can remember the claimant's activities on the day the injury was supposed to have occurred cannot be found. The use of a weekly noninjury statement tends to discourage late reporting.

The employer should be aware, however, that the employee has the right, under workers' compensation law, to report an injury up to one year after the date of the alleged injury. The purpose of this law is to allow a claimant to receive benefits for an injury whose initial symptoms did not indicate a long-term degeneration of function. Unfortunately, many legitimate back-related injuries will not present full symptomatic evidence until some time after the initial injury.

When employees sign a weekly noninjury statement, they are not giving up the right to file a late workers' compensation claim, but it is likly that the claim will be thoroughly investigated by the insurance carrier. Employers should make it clear to employees that the purpose of the weekly statement is to remind employees to report any injury, regardless of how minor it may seem, to ensure that they will receive full benefits should the injury turn out to be serious.

Some employers fear that using a weekly noninjury statement will cause greater abuse of the system by unscrupulous individuals. In fact, it will reduce abuse because the individual must conjure up a careful explanation of an injury to pass the scrutiny of a thorough investigation of witnesses who are quite likely to remember the claimant's activities. This in itself, as noted above, is an effective deterrent to the invalid claim.

Job Safety Analysis

A job safety analysis is normally performed in conjunction with the development of training checklists. However, such an analysis may also be important under other conditions. For example, a loader operator, skilled and thoroughly trained, is operating a loader at a construction site with steep dropoffs in areas where the loader will be operating. Prior to directing the loader operator to work in this hazardous location, the job site superintendent would conduct a job safety analysis to determine the operating parameters and areas where extra caution will be needed. The superintendent would meet with the loader operator and his helpers, discuss the work to be performed, the hazards to be avoided, and the proper operating procedures to be followed. This might include determining where dump trucks are to be parked and specifically where the loader is to operate.

The job safety analysis does not necessarily require a form. However, the superintendent should "walk through" the planned operation, documenting the hazards and the procedures needed to deal with the hazards. Subsequently, the documentation should be used to ensure that all pertinent points are covered in the safety meeting with the operator and helpers. For proof of such a meeting, the documentation should be signed by all present at the meeting or individual counseling session.

It should never be assumed that an experienced operator will perform a job safety analysis prior to performing the assigned work. Accident investigations are replete with statements from injured parties indicating that they "knew they should not have performed the operation as they did because it would lead to an accident." Superintendents should be cognizant of the fact that criminal prosecution has ensued against individual superintendents because they directed a worker to perform a task at which the worker was subsequently killed due to improper procedures that could have been avoided by proper supervision. Without documentation, the superintendent will have no proof that every effort was made to counsel the employee in safe operating procedures for the assigned task.

COMMON ILLNESSES AND CONDITIONS

Carpel Tunnel Syndrome

Carpel tunnel syndrome (CTS) is a condition affecting the median nerve in the hand. It results in pain, numbness, tingling sensations, and loss of use of the hands and fingers. These effects are caused by excessive pressure on the nerves entering the hand through the wrist via the carpel tunnel. This pressure can be due to inflammation of the tendons that pass through the wrist to the middle and ring fingers. Pressure can also be caused by damage to the muscles and/or bones surrounding the tunnel.

CTS can lead to other injuries. Afflicted workers may not be able to sense heat and cold properly, or may drop materials and tools on themselves or others due to loss of feeling in the hands. Carpel tunnel syndrome has been related to a number of causes. The primary occupational causes include holding the wrist in an unnatural position while:

- Performing work involving repetitive motion
- Repeatedly grasping objects tightly
- Using hand-held vibrating machinery

CTS can also be caused by a direct blow to the hand, and personal factors can predispose an individual to CTS. These include pregnancy, gynecological surgery, and various diseases and vitamin deficiency.

Tenosynovitis

Tendons are thin fibers of tissue that attach muscles to bones. The movements of the fingers are controlled by tendons attached between the fingers and muscles in the forearms. These tendons pass through lubricated sheaths. Tenosynovitis is the inflammation of these sheaths. This inflammation can cause pain, swelling, tenderness, cracking sounds, and loss of movement. Inflammation can result from repetitive over-exertion of muscles, or stretching, or tearing of the tendon. Tenosynovitis can also be caused by performing a job the worker is not used to, or working in unusual positions.

The most common areas affected by tenosynovitis are the back of the wrist, the side of the wrist near the palm, the base of the palm, and the palm side of the fingers. Tenosynovitis can occur anywhere tendons connect, but is most common at wrist, elbow, shoulder, and knees.

De Quervain's Disease

De Quervain's disease is an inflammation of the tendons connected to the thumb, and is a form of tenosynovitis. This condition has been related to tasks involving repeated inward hand motions with a firm grip.

Trigger Finger

A form of tenosynovitis, trigger finger is a condition imposed when any finger other than the thumb must frequently be flexed against resistance.

Tennis Elbow

Sometimes called epicondylitis, this form of tendonitis is an inflammation reaction of tissues in the elbow region. In an industrial environment it may be due to an effort requiring a repetitive or violent hand extension. Shock type vibration through the arm can also cause tennis elbow. It can be avoided by ensuring that rotation of the tool or machine coincides with the natural rotation of the forearm.

Raynaud's Syndrome

Raynaud's syndrome is characterized by feelings of numbness and coldness in the fingers. There is also lack of muscle strength and finger control. The fingers can become pale, and there is loss of sensitivity to heat and cold. The condition is caused by damage to the blood vessels in the hands resulting from vibration. The effect is generally reversible, except in the most extreme cases. The use of vibrating hand tools, including chainsaws, rotary grinders, and pneumatic tools, has been related to the disease.

Gloves

Improperly fitted work gloves may increase the risk of cumulative trauma. If the glove fits too tightly around the wrist, it will increase the pressure on the carpal tunnel. An improperly fitted work glove can also make it necessary for an employee to grip a tool harder, which can increase stress on the carpel tunnel in the wrist and on the tendon sheaths throughout the body.

Gloves should not be worn while working around rotating equipment such as drills, lathes, milling machines, and similar equipment. A glove can be snagged by the machine with enough force to tear a thumb or finger completely off the hand.

Cold

Working in low temperatures can increase the risk of CTS. Low temperatures can reduce feeling in the hand, causing the employee to feel that the tool is not being held tightly enough and increasing stress on the carpel tunnel. An overly tight grip can also increase the vibration transmitted from the tool.

Tools

The stress on the carpel tunnel can be increased by improperly sized hand tools. If the employee must press the handle of the tool into the center of the palm, it can compress the median nerve and cause pressure in the carpel tunnel. An improperly shaped tool handle may force an employee to work with the wrist bent in an unnatural position, which increases the risk of tenosynovitis and CTS. Substitution or modification of hand tools can reduce this risk of CTS, tenosynovitis, and so forth. The objectives of tool substitution or modification are to:

- Eliminate or reduce the need to bend the wrist while working with the tool.
- Reduce the force applied by the worker when using the tool.
- Reduce the vibration transmitted to the hand.

A tool with a properly bent handle can reduce the need to bend the wrist. Tool handles should be large enough to span the palm of the hand and rest on the muscle pads surrounding the palm to prevent pressure on the median nerve. Substitution of a straight handled tool for a tool with the handle at a right angle may reduce CTS risk in some circumstances.

The addition of a flange to a tool can reduce the force needed to use it. The employee can push or pull against the flange, rather than being required to squeeze the handle to push or pull the tool. The addition of a flange can also make the tool feel more secure and reduce the feeling that the tool must be gripped tightly.

The force required to operate the tool can be reduced by replacing trigger controls held down by one finger with levers operated by four fingers, foot controls, or automatic switching.

The occurrence of Raynaud's syndrome and CTS caused by vibration of hand tools can be reduced by proper selection of tools. Tools can be fitted with cushioned grips to dampen vibration. However, caution must be used when retrofitting cushioned grips, as the change can alter the frequency of the vibration, actually making the exposure worse.

Padding of sharp corners and edges and cushioned arm rests can also help reduce point stresses. The use of gloves similar to the type used in bowling to keep the wrist straight may be helpful in some instances.

In many cases, rotation of work stations to avoid vibration or odd angle wrist exposure for long periods of time is the most beneficial. This solution creates a work force with greater flexibility and can be an additional asset when workers are absent due to illness.

DEALING WITH HAZARDOUS SUBSTANCES

Hazard Communication Standard

The following brief discussion presents only an outline of the procedures necessary to comply with employee right-to-know laws. Later in this chapter, and in Appendix B the reader will find materials and information covering this subject in detail.

The Hazard Communication Standard states that every employer, regardless of size or degree of employee exposure, must inform employees of all hazardous substances with which they are working or will be working in the future. Furthermore, every employer must train employees in the proper procedures for working safely with such substances and supply all necessary protective equipment recommended by the substance manufacturer's material safety data sheet.

The law allows civil penalties to be assessed against any employer not in compliance, and criminal prosecution of an employer for the death or serious injury of an employee due to noncompliance or negligence.

Communication Guidelines

The hazardous substances program which is part of your safety program should cover the following points:

- A written inventory of all substances and materials used by your employees. This inventory must be kept current.
- Material safety data sheets obtained from the suppliers, distributors, or manufacturers of the substances and materials used in your operation.
- Personal protective equipment available to your employees as recommended by the material safety data sheets. Keep a current inventory of all personal protective equipment. Require all employees to wear the appropriate protective equipment and enforce these requirements through normal incentive and disciplinary action.
- Create material safety data sheet binders which are appropriately placed and readily available to any employee who desires the information. If your company has several divisions which are physically separated, it is allowable to have a master binder at a central location, available to all employees, and minibinders in other locations that contain data sheets appropriate to substances handled in those locations. If there is an interchange of hazardous materials between various locations, there must be appropriate redundancy.
- Hold safety meetings and individual training sessions to inform employees of the hazardous substances and how to deal with them under normal and emergency circumstances. Make certain to document all safety meetings and/or training sessions with dated attendance rosters and employee signatures.
- Make certain that all containers are appropriately labeled with approved hazardous substance labels. If your old containers lack these labels, new ones may be obtained from the supplier, distributor, or manufacturer.
- State in writing that you have done the above and indicate the method of updating information and recurrent training you intend to follow. Place this information in the front of your material safety data sheet master binder.

Information Sources

Sources of information on compliance with the Hazard Communication Standard and related laws:

- California Chamber of Commerce (800-331-8877) Book: *Hazardous Materials Handbook,* $25 (Chemicals, Laws, Agencies); Hazardous Communication Handbook, $30 (state/Fed law); Hazardous Substance Communication Act Kit, 18.00.
- OSHA 3105 Hazardous Communication Compliance Kit, GPO Order # 929-022-00000-9. Superintendent of Documents, US Government Printing Office, Washington DC, 20402-9325. 202-783-3238 with credit card.
- Hazardous substance software - MSDS Program Mgr, Genium Publishing Co., Rm 208, 1145 Catalyn St., Schenectady, N.Y. 12303 -1836 518-377-8854
- SARA: SARA Manual for field consulting, 431 Lenox Court, Pleasant Hill, CA 94523 ($37)
- SARA III - Community Right To Know Manual - $249 with 12-month updates. 1-800-424-2959 Thompson Publishing Company, Subscription Service Center, PO Box 76927, Washington DC, 20077-4690. Tel. 202-554-1404.

Note: SARA III is the public/community counterpart to the Hazard Communication Standard. Compliance requires registration of the employer's emergency plan in the event of an unexpected spill or release of hazardous substances. It also requires registration of the substances used in the operation. This law is enforced by one or more local agencies designated by the state and/or local community. In general, it is enforced by local hazardous substances response teams attached to firefighting agencies.

PROGRAM EVALUATION

Many employers have portions of the loss control program suggested in this book in place. Perhaps they are wondering how effective their programs are relative to the total program suggested herein. Therefore, a scorable checklist (Exhibit 11-1) is provided so that employers may evaluate the effectiveness of their programs.

UNDERWRITING CRITERIA

Although every individual insurance carrier has its own underwriting guidelines, there are similarities among all carriers. The

LOSS CONTROL CHECKLIST

	Score	Weighted %
Written framework:		
Safety policy	2	.02%
Rules and regulations	5	.04%
Signed statements of compliance	6	.05%
Hiring policy:		
Applications filled out	10	.10%
Reference checks conducted	15	.15%
Preemployment physicals	10	.10%
Careful subjective selection	15	.14%
Safety program:		
Weekly safety meetings	10	.10%
Bimonthly meetings	5	.05%
Monthly meetings	1	.01%
Weekly safety inspections	10	.10%
Bimonthly inspections	5	.05%
Monthly inspections	1	.01%
Written accident investigation with corrective action and witness statements	5	.05%
Informal report	1	.01%
Claims mangement:		
Designated physician program	5	.05%
No designated physician program	1	.01%
Employer-paid first aid	5	.05%
Availability of loss control consultant	2	.02%

The raw score must be adjusted by a weighted percentage. Example: Score by category × % by category = effect (Score) 52 × (weighted percent) 52% = 27.04% effectiveness

Exhibit 11-1

following questions are normally asked by all insurance company underwriters when considering acceptance of a given risk. The questions will normally be covered in an underwriting survey, also known as an insurance inspection. The survey or inspection will be conducted by a member of the insurance company's loss control department, or in some cases by an independent inspector.

How the employer answers these questions both in content and attitude will have a significant impact on whether or not the carrier will accept the risk and the competitiveness of the quote offered.

What Is the Nature of the Business?   The underwriter is looking for a clear discription of the operations, including products produced, machinery used, and methods of distribution. Most underwriters have never worked in the field and often have no idea of what an operation really looks like; unfortunately they may have preset ideas about the quality of the operation based on insurance industry prejudices.

The field representative with whom the employer is talking may be equally uninformed. It is therefore important for the employer to describe carefully all aspects of the operation, with special emphasis on the safety precautions and the care and concern for employees. Never assume that your agent has adequately described your operation in his or her narrative. Even when this is the case, insurance companies tend to discount the information because they assume the agent will fail to tell them about critical defects in the underwriting profile of the operation in order to improve the chances of receiving a competitive quote.

When showing a field representative around the operation, make certain to point out all the safety features. Name and describe the machinery and tools in use. Never assume the field representative knows what he or she is looking at, or its method or purpose of operation.

How Many Locations? Where Are They?   This is important to an underwriter to ensure that they are able to cover all locales. Not all insurance companies are licensed to operate in all states, or internationally.

Any Subsidiaries? An underwriter is concerned that the company not cover a hazardous subsidiary under the guise of the primary operation. Hiding this information will only lead to problems when the full operation comes to the attention of the underwriter. Under most insurance contracts, failure to disclose, in good faith, the full nature of all operations, including subsidiaries, may be grounds for immediate cancellation or voiding of the original coverage. This is especially critical with workers' compensation and general liability insurance, because claims may be successfully submitted months or years after an event occurs.

Financial Condition? Obviously no one is going to admit to being in deep water financially. Underwriters can and will access financial data reports on a prospective risk, but many employers will not provide accurate data to financial databases because of a desire for privacy and because many database firms will sell such information to virtually anyone. However, an employer should be prepared to provide an up-to-date financial statement to the underwriter if requested. Underwriters are concerned about whether or not an employer will pay the premium on time. The competitiveness of the quote will be determined to some extent by their confidence in the financial status of the employer.

Type of Ownership? Type of ownership is important for several reasons, but mostly because sole proprietorship owners may not insure themselves for workers' compensation insurance, whereas corporate officers are employees of the corporation and may insure themselves if they so desire. Corporate officers who do not take advantage of this option are depriving themselves of one of the least expensive forms of disability insurance.

The question is also important because underwriters prefer owner/principals who are involved in the daily management of the business. Their thinking is that greater concern for the well-being of the employees will be shown by an active owner.

Names and Duties of Principals? This question is in part relative to the one above, but also just confirms the information provided on an application.

Years in Business?   In general, underwriters prefer established businesses with a successful history. Quotes for new businesses are often less competitive than those for established ones.

Attitude toward Loss Control Programs and Safety?   This is a subjective question which will not be asked by the field representative. Your attitude, courtesy, and presentation, along with the status of your loss control program, will provide the answer to this question. A negative answer will significantly affect the underwriter's decision.

Use Subcontractors?   Underwriters are concerned about covering employees for which they have not been receiving premiums. Subcontractors, in the eyes of workers' compensation law, are your employees if they are injured while working for you and have no workers' compensation insurance of their own.

Many insurance companies will simply not offer coverage to general contractors because of the many subcontractors they employ. This problem may be overcome by maintaining accurate records of subcontractors' certificates of insurance and developing a method of ensuring the certificates remain in force.

Since small one-man artisan subcontractors cannot get workers' compensation coverage for themselves, the employer must report their remuneration as payroll for premium purposes. If these controls can be shown to the field representative, the underwriter will have confidence in providing a quote.

Used as Subcontractors?   This question really applies to general liability insurance but may be asked for workers' compensation insurance as well.

Require Certificates of Insurance from Subs?   As indicated above, this is a critical question that needs to be answered thoroughly.

Number of Employees?   The estimated annual premium determines the deposit which will be charged by the insurance carrier at the time a workers' compensation policy is written. Unscrupulous agents will attempt to compete with an employer's current agent by underestimating payrolls. This allows the agent to offer the employer a substantially reduced deposit, which will then be touted as confirmation of the competitiveness of the quote. Underwriters are well aware of this tactic and will "come in the back door" by estimating payrolls via number of employees. If deception is suspected they will refuse to quote or raise the quote accordingly.

Since all workers' compensation insurance is state-regulated, any employer quoted substantial deposit premium differences should be wary of the payroll base estimated by the agent providing the quote. Most insurance agencies will offer deposit premium rollover options to preferred customers. However, underestimated payrolls create substantial additional deposit premiums due at renewal and negate the advantage of deposit rollover plans.

Type of Pay Scale?   Underwriters are very concerned about the underpaid or minimum wage employee. This is because the workers' compensation lost wage replacement formula is designed to replace the employee's net wage with a minimum base. In some instances this minimum base, which is tax free to the injured employee, is greater than the wage the employee is receiving after taxes.

Employers who use minimum wage employees need to emphasize their loss control efforts and incentive programs to overcome this built-in stigma.

Average Age?   This question is really discriminatory and is generally answered by field representative observation. The reason for the question revolves around statistics which indicate that older workers and younger workers are involved in the majority of work-related injuries. Therefore, an underwriter wants to see a good mix of employee ages, with the ideal average age being about 35 with present statistical data.

Number of Part-time Workers?   Here again, the minimum lost wage replacement formula generates underwriting concern. A part-time employee may take home more money under a fake injury than can be earned doing the job for which he or she was hired.

Frequency of Overtime? Overtime leads to fatigue and fatigue leads to injury. Underwriters are looking for employers with reasonable overtime practices and good supervisory control. Some employees will work all the overtime they can, even to their own detriment.

Experienced? Statistically, experienced workers are injured far less often than inexperienced workers.

Training Program? If inexperienced workers are hired, the underwriter wants to see a well-documented training program.

Relatives Employed? This question seems to address the concern that relatives are often the ones who disobey work rules with impunity. This not only increases the risk of injury to them, but defeats the effects of loss control efforts on other employees.

Seasonal? Seasonal employees represent an increased risk for submission of invalid claims. These will normally be turned in just prior to the expected layoff. Employers in this situation should gear their loss control efforts accordingly. The enlightened employer will make an effort to help the employee find temporary employment for the slow season if at all possible.

Union? Union operations almost always preclude thorough preemployment screening. Here the employer's relationship with the union and continuity of employees is important. The employer who is calling for a new crew every other week is very suspect as a quality risk.

Planned Layoffs? As indicated above under seasonal work.

Absenteeism? The underwriter is concerned primarily with both the employer-employee relationship and the repetitiveness of work duties. Repetitive duties without satisfactory loss control lead to boredom and accidents. High absenteeism may be a symptom of boredom, or poor employer-employee rapport which leads to invalid claims.

How Are Employees Hired?   Underwriters like to see centralized hiring policies with thorough employee screening because that is the foundation of good loss control.

Number of Shifts?   The concern is for late shift supervision. Operations with one or two employees working alone at night are suspect because of the opportunity for one employee to sleep while the other is working. If the working employee is injured, who will come to his or her aid? Ditto for the lone employee.

Any Interchange of Labor?   Workers' compensation job classifications are based on most hazardous exposure profiles. Some employers will attempt to beat the system by listing high-exposure employees under low-exposure classifications where such options exist within the operation. This situation may be exposed at the end-of-year audit, or when a lower-classified employee is injured doing a higher-classified job. Unfortunately, the insurance company will still have covered that employee for too little premium for the actual exposure. Insurance companies will charge retroactive additional premiums when such improper classification is uncovered. Insurance companies will make every effort to place lower-classified employees into higher-classified positions when the end of the policy year audit is performed. Employers must be sure their payroll records show appropriate separation of payrolls by hours employed to avoid additional premium being assessed at the end of the policy year.

Kinds of Accidents in the Past Year?   This is an "honesty" question. Most underwriters will not even quote a piece of business without seeing loss runs for at least three years from the employer's prior carriers.

Many employers fail this test because they try to downplay prior losses. There is no gain in this, as the underwriter will have the information in writing from the prior carriers. And while they do not expect the employer to remember every single claim, they do expect some degree of honesty here.

Any Claims over $10,000?   As noted above.

Corrective Actions Taken?   Here the employer has a chance to improve its image in the eyes of the underwriter concerning prior losses. An employer who has learned from prior losses, taken corrective action, and solved the problem will greatly enhance the desirability of the risk.

Future Loss Probability?   This is a subjective question answered by the field representative. The answer will depend greatly upon the employer's explanation of corrective action and the effectiveness in regard to the employer's loss control program.

OSHA 200 Log Kept?   Again, some employers try to hide prior losses by not documenting them, as required by law. This is foolish, to say the least. Typically a field representative who knows his or her job will ask the employer about prior losses and then ask to see the OSHA 200 log. Discrepancies between the verbal response and documentation, or the lack thereof, will be noted.

Written Safety Policy?   The questions below are designed to determine the extent of the employer's loss control efforts both for underwriting purposes and to help the insurance company's loss control department estimate the level of service required.
    Loss control service is assigned relative to premium size. If the service estimated as required is greater than the premium size will allow, there is a good chance the underwriter will pass on quoting the account.

* Is there a designated safety director?
* Describe supervisor safety duties.
  Safety committee?
* Are accident investigations done?
* Are safety inspections conducted?
* Are medical facilities designated? First aid? Nurse?
* Are preemployment physicals conducted?
* Is there an incentive program?

Hazards Associated with Operations?   This question is answered by the field representative based upon observation and the employer's description of the operations.

MSDS Program in Effect? As noted earlier in the chapter, a hazardous substance communications program is a matter of law.

Storage of Flammables? Fire Protection? This question is also found on general liability and fire surveys. Underwriters are concerned about the storage of flammables both from an employee injury standpoint should a fire start, and for property damage reasons.

If an insured company suffers a serious fire, the business will be shut down, at least temporarily, and anticpated premium will be lost. Underwriters do not want to lose premium dollars.

Environmental Exposures? This question is primarily found on general liability surveys because of the many local ordinances as well as federal laws addressing these concerns. However, hazards to the environment are also generally hazards to workers as well.

Worker Transportation? Company Aircraft? Group transportation of workers is always of concern to underwriters because of the catastrophic potential. An employer should be prepared to disclose the precautions taken to avoid such an event. The same concern holds true for aircraft, with the added concern that aircraft are often flown by owners who are subsequently killed if the craft goes down. Apart from the workers' compensation loss that may occur, the underwriter is worried about the viability of the operation following such an event and of course collection of premiums due.

Many companies simply will not quote where aircraft are involved. Those that will are looking for aircraft flown by professional pilots with much time in the type of aircraft being used. The craft must be professionally maintained, and not used for charter. Twin-engine aircraft are more acceptable than single-engine aircraft. Short-distance flights, less than 400 air miles, are good. Beyond this range, insurers seem to think commercial flights are more appropriate.

Use of Motorcycles, or ATVs? These vehicles are of concern because of the high injury rates.

Building and Approximate Area?   Here the underwriter is concerned about work space, as congestion leads to higher injury rates. The field representative will make a subjective judgment.

Housekeeping?   Housekeeping is a very important item because it is indicative of the employer's organization and concern. Poor housekeeping goes hand in hand with high accident rates. The reason is both physical and psychological. Physically, poor housekeeping leads to trip and fall, and slip and fall injuries. Psychologically, poor housekeeping creates an atmosphere in which employees learn to ignore clutter. Soon they begin to ignore other safety rules as well, and ultimately these poor work habits lead to injury. Most field representatives will prepare a negative report when housekeeping is not satisfactory.

Vehicles? DMV Checks?   Underwriters are concerned about employee injuries from vehicular accidents. Statistically these are of high frequency and severity, so they are interested in the maintenance of the fleet, use of personal vehicles and control of their maintenance, as well as the driving records of employees driving for the company.

Preventive Maintenance?   This question applies to both vehicles and machinery. An employer who always waits for a machine to go down before doing repairs will have more frequent injuries than one who has an ongoing maintenance program. This precept parallels good housekeeping. Additionally, the underwriter is concerned about maintenance procedures, especially in regard to lock-out procedures.

The OSHA Form 200

By law each employer must keep a record of all reportable work-related injuries. However, if an employer has more than 10 employees, the record must be kept on a form prescribed by the *Federal* Occupational Safety and Health Administration (Fed-OSHA) known as the OSHA Form 200.

OSHA Form 200 is obtainable from any Fed-OSHA field office, which will be listed in the telephone directory under U.S. Government Offices. Or it may be obtained from:

Fed-OSHA, Publications Clerk, 71 Stevenson Street, San Francisco, CA 94105.

The form is self-explanatory. It must be posted by employers with 10 or more employees in a place where employee notices are normally posted between February 1 and March 1 each year. The posting covers the prior year's injuries.

Employers classified as Retail Trades, Finance, Insurance and Real Estate, and some Service Industries (SIC codes 71, 72,73,74,77,78) are exempt.

All employees must report to Fed-OSHA any fatalities that result from work-related injuries within 48 hours. Make certain to check state OSHA regulations, as fatalities and catastrophes may require less than 48-hour notice in certain states. Certain states may also require reporting by otherwise exempt classifications.

TOOLS FOR MONITORING LOSS CONTROL PROGRESS

FREQUENCY RATES

Each year, the Department of Labor Statistics publishes a list of Accident Frequency Rates correlated to Standard Industrial Code classifications. These statistics are normally two years behind current frequency rates due to the time required to collect and calculate the frequency rate for each individual classification.

Accident Frequency Rates provide a benchmark against which to measure an individual employer's accident frequency. National frequency rates are based on statistical data generated by all reportable accidents incurred by virtually all employers within the United States. A characteristic phenomenon of statistics is that the broader the statistical base, the more relevant the numerical computations and the more accurate the statistical predictions. Therefore, if all framing contractors in the United States develop a frequency rate of 11 and an individual employer develops a frequency rate of 14, it is obvious that the particular employer needs to improve loss control program effectiveness.

Frequency rates are based upon 100 employees working 40

hours per week for one year. In developing the formula, statisticians have made adjustments to allow applicability of the formula regardless of the number of employees employed by any given employer. The basic formula is this: The number of accidents incurred multiplied by 200,000 and then divided by the actual man-hours worked by all employees for any given employer. For example,

    15   employees
     3   accidents
35,000   man-hours worked (includes 5, 000 hours of overtime)

$3 \times 200,000 = 600,000 \div 35,000 = 17.1$

If the national average for this particular type of employer is 11, the formula can be reversed to determine how many accidents the employer should have had to meet the national average:

$$11 \times 35,000 = 385,000 \div 200,000 = 1.925.$$

Realistically this tells us that this particular employer should have had no more than 2 reportable (lost time, or medical treatment other than first aid) accidents during the preceding year.

Reversing the formula is very important for the small to medium employer because Labor Department statistics are affected by the massive size of a few employers in certain industries, particularly in manufacturing and some construction classifications. In the example above, a frequency rate of 17.1 seems very high compared to the national average of 11. When the formula is reversed, we find we are looking at the difference of one additional accident for this particular employer.

Many employers have very few serious accidents and may become complacent as a result. Employers who wish to use Accident Frequency Rate trends to monitor the effectiveness of their loss control programs need to make two separate calculations, one using reportable accidents for comparison to national averages and another using all accidents and near accidents for tracking their own individual trends on a year-to-year basis.

Remember that Accident Frequency Rates fail to take into consideration the severity of each accident. For example, if 5 people fall off a two-story scaffold while working for a very large employer, the employer's accident frequency rate may not be significantly affected. However, from a loss control point of view no scaffold fall is acceptable. Accident frequency rates therefore do not indicate how effective a loss control program is in preventing severe accidents, but they are useful in demonstrating relative trends.

Frequency rates are useful as loss control tools when they are used to track accidents and near accidents for a given employer over a 5 year or longer period without regard to national averages. If the trend is up, the employer needs to improve loss control efforts.

1984	11 employees 1 accident 24,200 hours (includes overtime)	$1 \times 200k / 24,200 = 8.26$
1985	13 employees 1 accident 28,600 hours	$1 \times 200k / 28,600 = 6.99$
1986	15 employees 2 accidents 33,000 hours (includes overtime)	$2 \times 200k / 33,000 = 12.12$
1987	17 employees 2 accidents 34,000 hours	$2 \times 200k / 34,000 = 11.76$
1988	15 employees 2 accidents 30,000 hours	$2 \times 200k / 30,000 = 13.33$

As can be seen from the example above, this employer has a trend of increased accident frequency relative to the number of man-hours worked.

The number of man-hours worked is the determining factor, not the number of employees, and so we find a deceptive element contained in this particular example. The years 1987 and 1988 contain no overtime, whereas the prior years do. It is important when tracking accident frequency rates to separate overtime from the formula if any year used has zero or nearly zero overtime. Let us adjust this example to zero overtime for all years:

1984	11 employees 1 accident 22,000 hours	$1 \times 200k / 22,000 = 9.09$
1985	13 employees 1 accident 26,000 hours	$1 \times 200k / 26,000 = 7.69$
1986	15 employees 2 accidents 30,000 hours	$2 \times 200k / 30,000 = 13.33$
1987	17 employees 2 accidents 34,000 hours	$2 \times 200k / 34,000 = 11.76$
1988	15 employees 2 accidents 30,000 hours	$2 \times 200k / 30,000 = 13.33$

When we compare, we find:

	1984	1985	1986	1987	1988
With overtime:	8.26	6.99	12.12	11.76	13.33
Without overtime:	9.09	7.69	13.33	11.76	13.33
Employees	11	13	15	17	15

Without overtime calculated into the formula, the 1986 frequency rate and the 1988 frequency rate are far more relevant, because in both years the same number of people were employed. (This comparison also demonstrates one major fallacy often used by employers to justify increased frequency rates. The employer will cite the fact that it has hired more employees and therefore has had a greater chance of accidents.) Accident frequency initially decreased each time staff was increased. This was probably due to the effect of good initial training. But as time went by, accident frequency increased even though staff decreased slightly. The increase in accident frequency was most likely the result of an inadequate loss control program.

Frequency rates can also be displayed as a graph to show loss control trends dramatically.

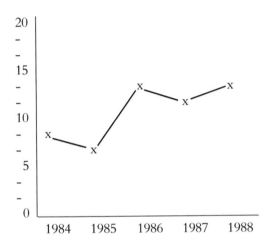

VARIANCE CHARTS

Another useful tool for tracking loss control trends by department is the variance chart. This chart or graph can be used for daily, weekly, or monthly display of accidents and near accidents.

ACCIDENTS AND NEAR ACCIDENTS

	Jan	Feb	March	April	June	July	August	Sept	Oct	Nov	Dec
Dept											
A	x	x	x			x		x			
B	x	x					x				
C	x		x								
D											
E				x							
F			x					x			x

A chart of this type can be used to correlate conditions that may be contributing factors to accidents. For instance, in the example above, the largest grouping of points occurred during the coldest months of the year. If the corresponding departments involved were exposed to cold weather, perhaps the environment was a contributing factor. Similar charts can track types of accidents, body parts involved, equipment involved, and other relevant data.

Again, in order for small employers to take advantage of statistical tools, all accidents and near accidents must be included in the database. The chart of greatest value to the employer will correlate loss control efforts with statistical accident and near accident data. Such a chart includes accident (A) and near accident (a) data, safety meetings (S), corrective action (C), loss control suggestions (s), and safety inspections (I).

Month:	January			
Week:	1	2	3	4
Dept:				
A	S	I/s	A	C
B	S			
C	I	S		
D			S	I
E				a
F		I/s	S	

A chart of this type, continued throughout the year with annotations, can be valuable in planning the next year's loss control efforts.

Annotations to the chart should include the topics of all safety meetings for the month by department, the loss control suggestions made as a result of safety inspections and if they were compiled within the month noted, or in a future month, the cause of any accident and the corrective action taken.

Maintaining the loss control correlation chart is

time-consuming and need be undertaken only if frequency rates for prior and current years indicate an upward trend. The chart can be adapted for tracking a number of variables and correlating their importance to the results of the employer's loss control efforts.

THE ONE-CARD SYSTEM

The one-card system can be used to suspense date all routine loss control activities, such as safety inspections, safety meetings, and recurrent training. The system consists of: a 3 × 5 file card box, 3 × 5 cards, 3 × 5 file card dividers showing the months of the year, weeks of the month, and optionally the days of the week. In other words, there is a divider for January, February, March, April, May, June, July, August, September, October, November, and December; plus the weeks of the month and the days of the week. The file cards may be used to list safety inspections, safety meetings, and recurrent training by department, by supervisor, or by individual.

For example: Let us assume that in July a safety inspection will be conducted in the tooling department, in September recurrent training is needed by four employees, and twice a year general plant safety meetings will be conducted in addition to regular bimonthly department safety meetings. Using the system, a card would be made up for each of these events indicating the type of event, topics of discussion, and individuals involved. Other pertinent notes can be added to the card, such as follow-up points from prior events. The card is then inserted in the appropriate month's divider slot. It can now be forgotten, because when the month comes up it will be retrieved as a reminder of the required event. At the beginning of the month, the person responsible for coordinating events will pull all the cards for the month and using a current calender, schedule the events into the appropriate weeks. At the beginning of each week, the cards for that week are pulled and assigned to the appropriate day.

Following the event, additional notes of reminder for the next occurrence of the event can be added to the card. Using a pencil facilitates addition and subtraction of notes following an event. The card is then moved forward into the appropriate month for the next occurrence of the event, and the system continues to operate indefinitely.

Employers with appropriate software for their computers can establish a similar system on the computer. Suspense date software is available for personal computers, but the use of such software is often more time-consuming than the hard copy system described above. The primary advantage of the one-card system is that it removes the need to remember the dates of important events and it provides continuity to the entire loss control program regardless of personnel changes. Often an employer establishes an excellent loss control program that is competently run by one individual. However, after that individual leaves, the program falls apart because the person replacing the former loss control person has no idea of what was being accomplished, or what was scheduled to be accomplished in the near or distant future. The one-card system eliminates this continuity problem because the next responsible person need only thumb through the file to get a good working picture of routine loss control events that need to occur.

RESOURCES

EDUCATIONAL MATERIALS & FILMS

Safety Meeting Outlines, Inc.
Box 294
Park Forest, IL 60466
312–481–6930
This company has excellent safety meeting topics on an annual subscription basis providing four topics per month. Approximately two-thirds of the topics are geared to the construction industry; the rest are general.

Krames Communications
312 90th St.
Daly City, CA 94015–1898
Produces small safety booklets on specific topics such as "Understanding and Preventing Heat Stress."

OSHA External Education Unit, Jim Lim, Jim Chung, Gerry
   Lombardo
415–557–2870

Technical Suppport, Fed OSHA, 415–995–5850

NIOSH Publication # 87–113, , Guide to Safety in Confined Spaces
513–533–8287.

Safety Films–Greater Los Angeles Chapter, National Safety Council
3450 Wilshire Blvd., Suite 700
Los Angeles, CA 90010

International Film Bureau Inc.
332 So. Michigan Ave.
Chicago, IL 60604–4382
312–427–4545. Rentals: $125.

National AudioVisual Center
8700 Edgeworth Drive
Capitol Heights, MD 20743
800–638–1300; information 301–763–1891.

Safety Training Encylcopedia—From Business and Legal Reports
800–553–4569
Cost: $143.
Demonstrates how to develop a safety program and provides related OSHA regulations.

Sub-Contractor Safety Study
CII, 3208 Red River St., #300
Austin, TX 78705–2650
512–471–4319

American Welding Society, Order Department
550 N.W. Lejeune Road
P.O. Box 351040
Miami, FL 33135
800–334–9353

OSHA Publications Office
200 Constitutional Ave. N.W., Rm. N3101
Washington DC 20210

AIDS ONE
800–423–5910
Cost: $22.50
Discusses legal ramifications and insurance concerns.

Posters

Associated General Contractors of California
3095 Beacon Blvd.
Sacramento, CA 95691
916–371–2422
Prop 65—hazardous warning signs

Clement Communications
800–345–8101
Creates unique posters, some with Herman character,
subscription basis.

HAZARDOUS SUBSTANCES

Used Oil Hotline (1–800–553–2962) lists businesses in
California willing to accept used oil from the public for
recycling.

California Waste Exchange
P.O. Box 942732
Sacramento, CA 94234
916–324–1807
Catalog of new technologies for waste management and
recycling, developing national database for research.

Chemical Hazard Communication Booklet and OSHA Book
   #3112: Air Contaminants—Permissible Exposure Limits
OSHA Publications, Rm. N-3101
Frances Perkins Bldg., 200 Constitution Avenue, N.W.
Washington, DC 20210

Dow Chemical Company
2020 Willard H. Dow Center
Midland, MI 48674
1–800–258–2436
Solvent handling booklets in Spanish and English and
posters.

Commercial Recyclers of Hazardous Wastes—Directory of
Industrial Recyclers
California Waste Exchange, Department of Health Services
P.O. Box 942732
Sacramento, CA 94234–7320
916–324–1807
Primarily California-based, although many recyclers are
national in scope.

SARA III: Community Right To Know Manual, $249 with
12 updates
Thompson Publishing Company
Subscription Service Center
P.O. Box 76927
Washington DC, 20077–4690
1–800–424–2959

NIOSH Current Intelligence Bulletins
4676 Columbia Parkway
Cincinnati, OH 45226–1998
513–533–8287.
These bulletins cover a variety of safety-related subjects
presenting the most current information.

Office of Toxic Substances: For Your Information Reports
EPA, Freedom of Information, A-101
Washington DC 20460
202–554–1404

"OSHA 3105 Hazardous Communication Compliance Kit"
GPO Order #929-022-00000-9
Superintendent of Documents
U.S. Government Printing Office
Washington DC 20402–9325
202–783–3238 (with credit card)

Hazardous Substance Software
MSDS Program Manager
Genium Publishing Co., Rm. 208
1145 Catalyn St.
Schenectady, NY 12303–1836
518–377–8854

Computer Aided Management of Emergency
OPs-SSA-Software-IBM Compatible
Ted Bielli
602–945–3299, or
National Safety Council
Foster City, CA 94404
415–341–5649
Provides information on CAMEO.

Prop 65—A Practical Guide for Compliance
916–441–7016
California only

Prop 65—Chemicals List
State of California, Health and Welfare Agency
1600 9th Street, Room 450
Sacramento, CA 95814 (California only)

SARA: SARA Manual
Field Consulting
431 Lenox Court
Pleasant Hill, CA 94523
$37.

Robert E. Brisbin and Associates
P.O. Box 341
Pismo Beach, CA 93449

NIOSH PUBLICATIONS
Available from NIOSH Current Intelligence Bulletins (see
p. 182). Call for availability and price.

Safe Maintenance Guide for Robotic Work Stations #88-108

Criteria for a Recommended Standard for Welding, Brazing,
   and Thermal Cutting #88-110A

Current Intelligence Bulletin Summaries #88-120

Recommendations for Occupational Safety and Health
   Standards 1988 #012

Occupational Diseases: A Guide to Their Recognition
   #017-033-00266-5

NIOSH/USCG/EPA OSHA Guidance Manual for
Hazardous Waste Activities #017-033-00419-6

Occupational Exposure to Hot Environments
#017-033-00423-4

Regulations, Recommendations, Assessments Extracted from
the Registry of Toxic Effects of Chemical Substances
#017-033-00424-2

Occupational Respiratory Diseases #017-033-00425-1

NIOSH Pocket Guide to Chemical Hazards
#017-033-0426-9

Stress Management in Work Settings #017-033-00428-5

Guide to Industrial Respiratory Protection #017-033-00430-7

Registry of Toxic Effects of Chemical Substances
#017-033-00431-5

A Guide to Safety in Confined Spaces #017-033-00432-3

HAZARDOUS SUBSTANCE TRAINING COURSES

Hazardous Waste Worker Training
415-642-5507

Pesticide Farm Safety Center
916-752-8939

EPA Accredited Asbestos Training Courses:
Laborer's Training Trust Fund for Southern California
714-763-4341

Med-Tox
Tustin, CA
714-259-0620

Napier & Assoc.
Torrance, CA
213-644-1924

National Institute of Asbestos and Hazardous Waste
Training
213-645-4516

TESTING

Safety Consciousness Psychological Profile Testing
London House
1550 Northwest Highway
Park Ridge, IL 60068
312–298–7311
This service has developed a testing profile for determining those people most psychologically prone to injury.

Air Quality Testing Equipment
Foxboro Analyzers
Smith & Dennison
Warren McGowan
1581 Industrial Parkway West, Suite 3
Hayward, CA 94544
415–782–9788

PERSONAL PROTECTIVE EQUIPMENT

Directories

Best's Safety Directory
A M Best Company
Ambest Road
Oldwick, NJ 08858
201–439–2200
Lists virtually all manufacturers of personal protective equipment, covering use, applicability under OSHA law, pictures, and ordering information. Cost approximately $30.

Backs

Health Pro
8203 Tomahawk Trail
Houston, TX 77050
713–458–7059
This company is a good source of weightlifter belts at reasonable prices.

Back Saver for Mechanics (when bending over to work on engine), $95.
Freisen Enterprises
P.O. Box 356
Virgil, Ontario, Canada, L0S 1T0

Gloves

Kevlar Gloves
Vegetable Growers Supply
1360 Merrill St.
Salinas, CA 93901
408–422–4822
$11.95

Golden Needles Knitting & Glove Co.
P.O. Box 803
Wilkesboro, NC 28697
919–667–5102
These gloves are made from the same material used in bullet-proof vests. They are more flexible than steel-mesh gloves and can be used for a variety of applications.

Slips and Falls

Non-Slip Floor Treatment
Paul Wagoner
Wagoner Floor Treatment
702–827–4466
24-hour number: 702–878–4768
This unique etching treatment for quarry tiles and tiles used in kitchens, halls, and entryways has been used by many hotels and restaurants with excellent results. Paul Wagoner has information on slip-and-fall accident reductions from major hotel and restaurant chains who have used his product.

REFERENCES

Government Reports

OSHA Facility and Catastrophe Investigations
National Technical Information Service
U.S. Department of Commerce
5285 Port Royal Road
Springfield, VA 22161
703–487–4600/487–4650

Books and Manuals

Best's Safety Guide—Vol. I & II
A M Best Company
Oldwick, New Jersey 08858

Supervisors Safety Manual (c 1978)
National Safety Council
Chicago, IL 60611
ISBN 0-87912-064-9

Security
Walter M. Strobl
Industrial Press
200 Madison Ave
New York, NY 10016
ISBN 0-8311-1101-1

OSHA Safety & Health Standards (29 CFR 1926/1910)
Revised 1987
U.S. Department of Labor OSHA 2207.

INDEX